FERTILE SOIL *in a*
BARREN LAND

an explorefaith.org book

FERTILE SOIL *in a* BARREN LAND

A DESERT ODYSSEY FOR THE SOUL

RENÉE MILLER

morehouse

HARRISBURG • LONDON

Copyright © 2005 by Renee Miller.

Unless otherwise noted, the Scripture quotations contained in the text are from the New Revised Standard Version Bible, © 1989 by the Division of Christian Education of the National Council of Churches of Christ in the U.S.A. Used by permission. All rights reserved.

The psalms contained herein are from the Psalter of the Book of Common Prayer, copyright © 1979 by the Church Hymnal Corporation, New York.

Morehouse Publishing, P.O. Box 1321, Harrisburg, PA 17105
Morehouse Publishing, The Tower Building, 11 York Road, London SE1 7NX
Morehouse Publishing is a Continuum imprint.

Cover design by Jim Booth

Library of Congress Cataloging-in Publication Data

Miller, Renee.
  Fertile soil in a barren land : a desert odyssey for the soul / Renee Miller.
    p. cm.
  ISBN 0-8192-2135-X (pbk.)
  1. Spiritual life—Christianity. 2. Wilderness (Theology) 3. Deserts—Religious aspects—Christianity. I. Title.
  BV4501.3.M547 2005
  248.4—dc22

                            2004026814

Printed in the United States of America

05 06 07 08 09 10   5 4 3 2 1

FOR RONALD,

*who led me through the true desert
where all is nothing and
nothing is all.*

Contents

explorefaith.org books
An Introduction

The book you hold in your hand says a lot about you. It reflects your yearning to forge a deep and meaningful relationship with God, to open yourself to the countless ways we can experience the holy, to embrace an image of the divine that frees your soul and fortifies your heart. It is a book published with the spiritual pilgrim in mind through a collaboration of Morehouse Publishing and the website explorefaith.org.

The pilgrim's path cannot be mapped beforehand. It moves toward the sacred with twists and turns unique to you alone. Explorefaith.org books honor the truth that we all discover the holy through different doorways, at different points in our lives. These books offer tools for your travels—resources to help you follow your soul's purest longings. Although their approach will change, their purpose remains constant. Our hope is that they will help clear the way for you, providing fruitful avenues for experiencing God's unceasing devotion and perfect love.

www.explorefaith.org

Spiritual Guidance for Anyone Seeking a Path to God

A non-profit website aimed at anyone interested in exploring spiritual issues, explorefaith.org provides an open, non-judgmental, private place for exploring your faith and deepening your connection to the sacred. Material on the site is rich and varied, created to highlight the wisdom of diverse faith traditions, while at the same time expressing the conviction that through Jesus Christ we can experience the heart of God. Tools for meditating with music, art, and poetry; essays about the spiritual meaning in popular books and first-run films; a daily devotional meditation; informative and challenging responses to questions we have all pondered; excerpts from publications with a spiritual message—all this and more is available online at explorefaith.org. As stated on the site's "Who We Are" page, explorefaith.org is deeply committed to the ongoing spiritual formation of people of all ages and all backgrounds, living in countries around the world. The simple goal is to help visitors navigate their journey in faith by providing rich and varied material about God, faith, and spirituality. That material focuses on a God of grace and compassion, whose chief characteristic is love.

You have the book, now try the website. Visit us at www.explorefaith.org. With its emphasis on God's infinite grace and the importance of experiencing the sacred, its openness and respect for different denominations and religions, and its ground-ing in the love of God expressed through Christianity, explore-faith.org can become a valued part of your faith-formation and on-going spiritual practice.

Introduction

There I was standing on the rim of the bathtub, holding my breath in stark terror at what was sitting on the bathroom floor—a dreaded desert scorpion. I was seventeen years old and this was not the first time I'd seen a scorpion, but seeing one up close still filled me with panic. When I could breathe and form a word, I called out to my fearless grandmother, who calmly came and, seeing the scorpion, very unceremoniously took a pink Kleenex from inside her shirtsleeve, picked up the deadly scorpion, and carried it outside. I heaved a hearty sigh of relief and stepped down from my bathtub perching place still wondering how my grandmother had the fortitude to deal with a scorpion with such aplomb. This was a great lesson that I would only begin to understand years of life later.

One of the first images that comes to mind whenever people are conversing about the desert is the nasty presence of scorpions. A nocturnal arthropod, scorpions are actually relatives of spiders. They feast on other insects and defend themselves by stinging and releasing venom on their would-be attackers. Surprisingly, only a few types of scorpions have venom that actually causes death in humans, but the sting and venom can cause pain and swelling, respiratory difficulty, and even convulsions. While scorpions are a normal part of desert life, they're by no means limited to the desert:

you can find them in many parts of the world and in lots of different environments. But still, along with rattlesnakes and roadrunners, they seem to have become a kind of "mascot" of desert terrain. In local tourist shops you can buy anything from rubber scorpions to real ones encased in acrylic paperweights. As comic as they can sometimes look, scorpions are dangerous and sometimes, even lethal. This is not, however, the critical lesson I've learned from them. The lesson I've learned after years of desert life is the clear truth that the desert itself can sting. Jumping on the rim of the bathtub to escape the scorpion has become, for me, a metaphor of my desire to avoid the inevitable stinging encounter with the unwieldy and unpredictable physical desert landscape—and the inner spiritual desert landscape, which is sometimes even more unwieldy and unpredictable.

Perhaps it's the very danger and mystery that causes such curiosity and fascination with desert terrain. Even if we haven't been in a physical desert, we've seen pictures of it. We've been moved by mysterious rock formations that emerge from the beautiful bare landscape, or the racy colors of the spring desert in bloom, or a desert sunset that stretches across an endless sky in colors as brilliant as the sun itself. But as beautiful as the bare desert can be, its beauty is raw and untamed. What was most impressive about my grandmother's treatment of the scorpion in the bathroom was that she wasn't stung, even though only a small piece of tissue separated her hand from the scorpion's venom. She taught me that the desert doesn't demand our fear but it will eschew our power. The desert requires that we approach without arrogance. It was the absence of arrogance that saved my grandmother from the scorpion's sting.

In this book, the physical desert terrain serves as the canvas upon which to paint a living picture of the desert reality in human life. This book is also about discovering the reality that the desert will be a part of our lives throughout the whole of our existence, whether or not we ever place our timid toes on hot sand or eat singed and fried prickly pear cactus for dinner. The desert is really an image, a symbol, for the times when our inner life feels as dead as a desert fossil merged into rock, when emptiness is screeching through our bones in vacuous echoes, when fear has wrapped around the arteries of our life and left us gasping for breath, when God is as absent and silent as the first shade of night descending, when danger lurks around every corner of our soul. In those "desert" times we'll taste darkness and emptiness. We'll feel the thirst that strikes with the power of a snake. We'll be pricked by truths as sharp as thorny cactus. We'll grapple with passionate pathos. But we'll always find hope as verdant as small wildflowers pushing through hard fissured desert sand to reach toward the sun. We'll encounter the desert in our own life and find a new life emerge within us.

While most of my life has been spent in the southwestern desert, this book was written outside that region. I had no idea that during the writing of it, I'd tread through an inner desert deeper than any I've known in the outside. As I entered that desert I hadn't expected, I felt the cataclysm of being turned inside out by the force of the desert wind, and it was the very writing itself that gave me the humility I needed to roll and bend as I was thrashed about. The inner spiritual desert that sweeps across our lives when we've been lolling through our days unaware may make us want to jump on the rim of the bathtub. But if we can simply calm our fear, become familiar with the wild tumult, and simply wait in patience and meekness, we'll find that the stinging desert tempest leads to the quiet and peaceful space where we can hear a living word from God.

CHAPTER 1

Silence

As the desert begins to wake from its slumber, and the flora and fauna greet the warm morning sun, the topography begins to reveal its unique and distinct features. Even when you know what the desert will look like at daybreak, there are always surprises. I'd been away from the desert for some years, returning only for short visits, and when I was finally able to make plans to return to live there again, I rented an apartment in a town that was only slightly familiar to me. My family and I arrived very late at night, after driving with all of our belongings for two days. It was so dark when we got there that we couldn't distinguish any of the desert's characteristics, except for the multitudinous and silent stars that hung above us like shiny jewels. We could only imagine the landscape as we remembered it. We climbed the steps to the apartment, laid out our sleeping bags, and wearily crawled in for a few hours of sleep. Already the deep silence had descended. It was as if the noise in my life that had become so customary, so usual, so ordinary had been captured and removed, leaving nothing but heavy, black stillness. I could hardly sleep because of my excitement about welcoming the dawn. I awoke just as the darkness was beginning to make way for the new morn. I edged my way out of the sleeping bag and was amazed to see the desert from every window. I stood in my own complete inner silence, voiceless—soundless—in the miracle before me. I stepped out onto the balcony and became surprisingly aware, as if for the first time, of the unique aspects of the desert: the expansive horizon, the monochromatic emptiness, the mountains in the distance so stolid and unmoving, the dry tasteless air, the neverending creosote bushes that dotted the landscape, and the poignant calm that rested over the land. That same calm crept into my soul, and I knew I had come home.

It's that great, great silence of the desert that draws me most, I suppose. It's the silence before time, before life, as we know it. It's the eternal language, the eternal space through which everything must come. It's the dwelling place of God. When dawn begins to emerge over the darkened horizon, it's a reminder that all of life is a birth from that silence, and when the day comes to an end and the curtain is drawn at the dramatic setting of the sun, it's a reminder that all of life will return to that silence.

We often find ourselves unbalanced because we feel a need for silence and yet we fear it at the same time. When stepping through the door into a church, for example, our soul longs for silence, and yet when there are moments of silence in a worship service, we squirm, we cough, we look at the service bulletin, and wonder why someone isn't saying or doing something. We're nervous about silence even as we hunger for it as the lone desert coyote hungers for solitude.

Everywhere we turn in our daily lives there is sound. We keep radios and televisions on for background "noise." We constantly cut through the silence like a ship cutting through the waters of a seemingly endless ocean, as if the great silence is so big, so ancient, that it has no need to accommodate itself to the intrusiveness of noise. In its maturity the silence can be supple enough to gently bend and move to allow the noise to pass through it unimpeded. Yet like a ship on the ocean, we risk getting lost in that sea of silence— being completely overcome by it. This fear wafts over us when we think of being still in the silence. What will happen to us? What will be required of us? What if we get bored? How can we face ourselves? What if we don't like what we see in ourselves?

When we have difficulty appreciating or embracing silence, the desert is the place to go. In the desert at dawn, the silence is so vast and palpable that there's no escape from it. There's a description of this immense quiet in the readings of the early Desert Fathers, those holy men of the fourth century who stepped away from the activity in the world in order to find God in the desert:

> This place was called Cellia, because of the number of cells there, scattered about the desert. Those who have already begun their training there and want to live a more remote life, stripped of external things, withdraw there. For this is the utter desert and the cells are divided from one another by so great a distance that no one can see his neighbour nor can any voice be heard. They live alone in their cells and there is a huge silence and a great quiet there. Only on Saturday and Sunday do they meet in church, and then they see each other face to face, as men restored to heaven.[1]

If we try to push through this kind of silence with our voice, or even our breathing, our sounds are nothing more than the slightest murmur that fades away almost unnoticed. This silence can be so relentless that seeing the face of another can seem the only respite from the terrible absence of all sound. On the other hand, the very enormity of the silence can work like a gentle massage on the soul. Slowly it becomes apparent that sound can clutter rather than clear the chaos of life, moving us from uneasiness to awe, from fear to reverence, from edginess to peace. We begin to see ourselves as we are—without pretension or untruth—and we begin to have a glimpse of eternity. We begin to realize that silence is the womb that gives us life. It cradles and nurtures us even when we're fighting against it.

We needn't fear that the silence will demand too much of us. The

---

1. Benedicta Ward, ed., *Daily Readings with the Desert Fathers* (Springfield, Ill.: Templegate Publishers, 1988), 39.

absolute silence that begins the dawn doesn't last for long. The desert begins to wake and move like the rest of life. Quail begin to scratch the sand, mourning doves coo their woeful tune, the dusty wind whispers across the dry desert floor. As the day is birthed, life slices through the massive hush. The sounds of the desert will continue throughout the day, but always at the end of the day there will be a return to the enormous cosmic silence.

You may feel that your life is routine. You may be engaged with work and family, fulfilling goals and expectations, dreaming and scheming about future plans and yet notice an inner disquiet creeping across your spirit. The desert dawn that comes with such silent power can come alive in your own soul, as you wake to the dawn of your own topography. It's a good exercise to take a few days to awaken in the dark silence and watch the dawn coming in the sky and in your soul. As you scan the geography of your inner life you'll begin to feel the movement of God within you. It may feel as though nothing ever changes in your life, but God's Spirit is pulsing within you, leading you to the recognition of the value and importance of your own soul. Like the desert when the evening vesture is gently laid aside, and the great silence begins its work of transformation, you will slowly wake up.

A Prayer Practice for Waking to the Dawn

Waken in the dark and settle yourself outside or near a window. It's counter-intuitive in this culture to wake while it's still dark. We're rarely aware anymore of the natural rhythm of an agricultural life. When you first begin this practice, it may seem difficult to pull yourself out of your warm sleeping place when light hasn't yet even brushed the sky. Be patient with yourself as your body begins to readjust to the pattern of getting up in the dark. Only a few experiences of being engulfed in the vast black silence will be needed to create a desire within you to arise even when it feels like the middle of the night.

Take a few moments to be aware of the darkness around you. There was a time when I found the dark oppressive. So much in our world and in our religious tradition leads us to see darkness as evil and light as goodness. We're accustomed to turning on the lights in a darkened room rather than sitting quietly in the blackness. We're more likely to take a walk in the briskness of a bright sunny morning than at nighttime under a moonless sky. Because we avoid darkness, it's good to begin this practice by noting how the darkness feels and what emotions rise in you as you feel yourself held in it. Pay attention to the feeling of not being able to detect shapes, of needing to grope your way through the room, of the desire to flick on the light switch, of the length of time needed for your eyes to begin to adjust to the darkness. Note also any emotional feelings that surface in you. Are you afraid, uneasy, puzzled by what you can't see? Do you feel any safety and security in the darkness because you're anonymous there?

Be aware of God's presence in you. It's not always easy to detect the presence of God within us. We're not sure what to look for, and we feel presumptuous or foolhardy to think we know what that presence is like. We may not think ourselves worthy for God to reside in us. We may be afraid to turn our awareness to that presence lest we find that we were mistaken and it's not there after all. We may be hesitant to acknowledge that presence because we're unwilling to face the demands that we assume will be placed upon us. Yet, as we begin to feel comfortable in the darkness, we've also begun to be attentive to God's company within us. To get a sense of this presence, close your eyes and feel the breath moving in and out of your nostrils. Place your hand over your heart and feel the beat of life within you. Let the breath and beat come together in a balanced rhythm and feel the spirit of God flowing quietly but certainly through you.

As the dawn begins to be born, imagine a curtain of darkness being raised from your soul. The other side of darkness is light. Just as nature provides a steady and dependable rhythm to the day, you can know that a similar rhythm is being lived out in your soul. As the sun slowly rises, the thick heavy drape of darkness is lifted and the light emerges, as if for the first time, nascent and fresh, no harshness to the transition, no favoring of one over the other, no sense of competition. It's a silent and balanced movement. As you watch that balanced movement, visualize the same drape of darkness being lifted from your soul and feel yourself being bathed in light. How gentle is the shift? Do you find yourself wanting to hurry the process? Is there any sense of uneasiness within you? Do you feel your soul becoming more buoyant, more lithe? Is there a willingness to "wake up" to the presence of God in your soul, as if for the first time? Sit patiently until the light has fully come in the sky, being aware of the subtle alterations that the same change brings in your own body.

Say a prayer of greeting to the day and to God. Every new day is a gift, and every new day ought to be honored with a greeting of welcome and thanksgiving. It's much too easy to take each new day for granted and move immediately to the tasks and responsibilities that await you, barely taking notice that a birth has occurred, a miracle has been unveiled, a sure and certain rhythm has given you a place of grounding yet again. Greet the newborn day as you would greet a brand new infant—with joy, with delight, with muted awe. As you offer your greeting to the dawn, greet the newness in your own soul as well. Just as each new day brings with it the possibility of another chance at life, so each new day brings with it the chance for your soul to be renewed.

As you sit still in the warm bath of the new day's light, take a few moments to let your heart speak its contents to the Holy One who has given the light, the renewal, the rhythm. Let the exchange between heaven and earth occur within your own soul as you offer to God a prayer of thanks for the wonder of another day of life.

Take five minutes to write your feelings in a journal. Journaling can feel like an onerous task after you've been engaged in mindful attention and reflection. You might even resist trying to capture on paper what's been so wordlessly experienced within. But the very action of scratching onto paper the feelings and impressions floating through your inner self helps to deepen and etch the experience on your soul. It has another purpose as well. It's a way of making the transition from meditation to lived life, of grounding and readying yourself for the day's activities. You don't need to write much. You don't need to write well. You don't need to capture every thought, every feeling. You simply need to take pen in hand and bring yourself into the present moment and record in short phrases what's occurred in you during the moments you've spent watching the earth change from night to day. The very action of writing is a way to give reverence to the beauty of your soul and the wonder of life.

CHAPTER 2

Solitude

The desert is, on its own, remote. It's vast enough to encompass cities, towns, mountains, communities of nomads, and individuals, and yet, it's remote. Its very enormity sets it apart from other more close-knit topographies. It stands immoveable, as if from before time, in its own solitude even though dry gulches and wayfarers, scorpions and sage, coyotes and creosote pepper its landscape. It provides a harsh hospitality to living things with the courage and perseverance to be immersed in the endless remoteness, the everlasting solitude.

We all know how the demands of work can both energize and deplete us. We know how the rigors of attending to the relationships in our lives can both reward and rob us. We know how the expectations of society can both nurture and negate us. Life has a way of encroaching on the edges of our soul until those edges are tattered and torn. It seems to have always been the case in my own life that when I'm feeling depleted, robbed, and negated, I flee to the desert to be embraced in its arms of solitude. I experience some of the same feelings the great prophet Elijah might have felt when he tried to escape not only the enemies who threatened to kill him, but who sought also to break away from the weariness and wastedness of his own limited self. Like Elijah, when I'm having a temper tantrum with life, I want only to be free of feeling overstuffed—overstuffed with people, noise, the media, stressors, and even my own puny self.

I remember one such recent escape. At first, I longed only to be rid of everything that was bearing down on me, and as I drove at dusk through the dusty desert I felt liberated because no one knew exactly where I was. The cell phone couldn't pick up a signal, there was no one waiting for me to show up somewhere, and I didn't have to do anything I didn't want to do. It was a glorious feeling and surely a self-centered one. But then, I began to feel strangely cradled in the massive solitude. As my car sped along at seventy miles an hour, the empty, silent land stretched its ocean of gritty sand all around me. With my window rolled down, the air, so squeezed of moisture, scratched the inside of my nostrils and constricted my throat. The sun, just beginning to descend, showed its willingness to quiet its relentless heat. The ground was tasteless, the sky full of flavor. Only an occasional automobile sped past me along the straight two-lane road, and in the landscape that seemed so bereft of pulsing existence, I realized suddenly that if I were to give up my life there in that nameless space, I would die happy and utterly fulfilled. I knew absolute contentment, knowing that I needed nothing more than to give myself to the immense solitude until it consumed me. Such solitude would be a most welcome and comfortable coffin. I knew that in reaching toward solitude, I had embraced both my life and my death.

There's something about solitude that helps us regain, restore, and renew our perspective. Somehow the vast emptiness that leaves us feeling we've been left without support actually makes it possible for us to reclaim the very lives we're trying to avoid. It's not unusual these days to complain mercilessly about the lack of balance we feel in our lives: how our days have become little more than repetitive 24-hour periods of robotic, frenetic, uncontrollable activity. As weary as we are with the lack of balance, we continue to fear and even shun solitude. Perhaps we worry that there will be no support for us in solitude. We actually seem to avoid the solitude by keeping our days full, our minds cramped, our souls submerged. The workdays run into one another without delineation and then when the weekend rolls around, we go out with friends, surf the Internet, or prowl around the mall. We fill every available moment with people, activities, or noise.

We do crave what might be called "solitude in small bites;" that is, some quiet time alone. It might be a simple hour of solitary reading or a warm bubble bath surrounded by candles. These small bites of solitude can seem like a precious and prized gift in the midst of an over-stressed life. But, as delicious as the small bites are, we're still timid about sitting down to a feast of solitude. We seem to know intuitively that that kind of solitude will turn us inside out and recast us in a new form, if not devour us completely. If we were to feast on a large platter of solitude, we'd find ourselves strangely uncomfortable. What would we do without our MP3 player? What if we got homesick? What if loneliness leered too menacingly at us? What would we do if there were no one to listen to but our own souls and heaven? What would we do if there were no one to share our concerns and complaints with but the invisible God? How long would it take us to get back to our civilized and measured days?

Surprisingly, the desert itself can support us as we tear down the thick bricks of fear that keep us from diving into the solitude that will expose our masks. The desert will test our mettle, purify our soul in the crucible of fire, uncover our illusions, challenge our assumptions, show our patterns of behavior for what they are, make us face ourselves as we never have before, and leave us breathless but finally truly breathing.

The coyote—one of the most familiar and enigmatic of the desert animals—is one such support. Traveling solo rather than in a pack like a wolf, the coyote risks the dangers of the desert as well as the hazards that solitude always carries. A mere twenty or so pounds, the coyote skulks through the dry, sandy grasses relying on the terrain itself to provide life and nourishment. Such solitariness develops the coyote in ways that running in a pack could never do. Listening for and detecting danger becomes much more critical and the coyote's ears develop a keen sense of hearing. Without relying on others to help provide food, the nose of the coyote becomes finely honed to help him in the discovery of nearby prey or the scent left by other coyotes that have marked out their territory. Coyotes can run up to forty miles an hour, partially because they're digitigrade: they walk with only their toes touching the ground. They creep around with a lightness on the earth that makes it appear as if they're hardly leaving any pressure where their feet have trod. When we're ready to step off the edge of our relational, conversational, communal life into the sea of solitude for a time of reshaping, this mysterious yet adaptable animal can help show us the value and rewards of such raw separation from the world of people that can sometimes feel so overwhelming. One of the first things that becomes apparent in extended periods of solitude is the sheer heaviness of the silence. More than merely masking noise, the looming silence is actually a womb where we can relearn the value and skill of listening. Our ears, like the coyote's, become more attuned to sound when we're dropped into that silence. In the desert such keen listening is imperative to avoid danger—from the scurry of a deadly scorpion to the rattle of the snake that can kill. But beyond the physical necessities of safety, desert solitude helps us begin to listen and hear the sounds we may have never heard, or perhaps have forgotten in the continual rush of our daily lives. We're amazed to hear the sounds of our own soul, and the whisper of heaven's voice, and the timorous tones that seek to crack our encrusted heart, and the quiet and steady beat of the earth itself. In that immense silence, we begin to hear the sounds of holiness that will prepare us for life back in the world of activity and people.

As our hearing becomes less intense in our everyday life in society, so our sense of smell becomes relegated simply to detecting and defining things. Just as the coyote's nose develops an acute sense of scent through a life of lone-ness, so when we go into desert solitude, we are abruptly aware of scents that have been hidden from us—if ever we knew them at all. It might be the grainy desert wind, the dryness of air before a rain, the pungent aroma of chapparal after the rain has come and gone. But such an acute smell of the landscape leads us to something much grander. We begin to see how even the nose is important in our life with God. We begin to detect odors that assure us of presence of God, and the presence of God begins to saturate us until God's scent flows through us for others. It is said of some of the Desert Fathers and Mothers that at the moment of their death, the room was filled with a sweet odor— as though even in the final moments of earthly life, it was important to bear the sweet scent of God. In desert solitude we develop the skill of smelling the presence of God, and when we return to the world of people, we can allow that scent to seep out of our own pores so that others can smell that same sweet odor.

Unlike the coyote, we are not digitigrade, but in desert solitude we do begin to move more softly, to tread more lightly, to leave less trace of where we've been. Walking lightly on the earth is not only a form of honoring the life-force that created the dust from which we all were made, but it is also the ultimate form of humility. In our workaday worlds, we want to make a difference and leave a mark, lest we die having contributed nothing, forgotten as a dry leaf dropped from an old tree on a brisk autumn morning. Desert solitude reminds us that life isn't about "us" as individuals. It is about the One who gave us that life. Whole societies of Native Americans came and went through the desert leaving nothing behind but the softest shape of their moccasin in shifting sand. Who were they? How did they live? What was their purpose in life? What contribution did they make? Why did they leave their habitations? Were they remembered by anyone? It seems like a hard humility—and it is. But, in desert solitude we become so drenched in that humility that when we return to the world of people and activity, we find ourselves more subdued, less self-absorbed, more willing to step onto the earth and into our relationships with greater tenderness. We are more able to give what we have to give without needing to leave an unmistakable impression of where we've been, what we've said, what we've done.

Yes, the demands of work can both energize and deplete us. The rigors of attending to the relationships in our lives can both reward and rob us. The expectations of society can both nurture and negate us. Life has a way of encroaching on the edges of our soul until those edges are tattered and torn. The deep of desert solitude calls. Heed her voice.

A Prayer Practice of Desert Solitude

Commit to a time. It seems odd to think that solitude should be scheduled, but because of the complexity of our lives and our almost natural inclination to avoid solitude, the first place to begin practicing desert solitude is to open the calendar and set aside a time to step out of the whirlwind of daily life into the world of silence and seclusion. You will probably notice that many excuses rise to the surface. The items on the calendar and the preparations needed to complete those items will eclipse the desire to commit to rearranging the schedule to accommodate the solitude that quietly beckons. The production of results is so highly prized in our culture that the notion of secluding ourselves away in a cocoon of nonproductivity seems a dreamy shadowland of possibility for others, but hardly practical for ourselves. When the excuses loom, try to listen to the whisper of the Spirit within you calling you to "come away and rest awhile." Take pen in hand, clear a day, or a week, or a month, or even a year and scratch time for solitude into the calendar. Then, observe the release, the relief, the refreshment that seem to waft over your soul once you lay the pen and calendar down. "Ah . . . ," your soul will say.

Plan the place. While desert solitude in a geographical desert may be ideal, it may not be realistic. Desert solitude is actually more expansive than a simple topography. As Franz Kafka wrote, "You do not need to leave your room." Or, as the early Desert Fathers relentlessly reminded their disciples, "Sit in your cell and your cell will teach you everything." The place you choose as your womb of desert seclusion can be as near to you as your own bedroom or as distant as the Himalayas. The actual physical space is not that important because the space is just the container within which you will be invited to descend into the protective and instructive embrace of the holy solitude for which your soul longs. If, however, you're unsure about the feasibility of staying in your own home, look in the phone book for a nearby convent or monastery. A small room in a place where holiness has been practiced for years and years will make it easier for you to hear the call of the Holy One who will be waiting for you there.

Pack lightly. It will be incredibly seductive to pack your bag with things that will fill the solitude you're entering. This is merely a feeble attempt by your mind to quiet the rising terror that you'll be bored, lonely, and unable to cope with the raggedness of being cut off from what is known, what is familiar, what characteristically fills your days and nights. You may know that you want solitude, but you will find yourself wanting to have possible diversions just in case the solitude is more demanding than you can bear. Resist the temptation to take things to occupy yourself. Instead, prepare for your isolated journey by choosing your favorite Bible—the one that feels and smells and reads like gold to you. Carefully place it in your bag with your meager provision of clothing. Then, go to a stationery store and purchase a personal journal that looks and feels like it's ready to hold your thoughts and conversations with God. Put it in the suitcase with your Bible. Choose a pen or pencil that you'll want to write with throughout the time of your solitariness. Resist the urge to take more than one pen! Then, close your suitcase. Nothing but Bible, journal and pen, clothes, and toiletries need accompany you into the place your soul is headed. All else that you need there will be given to you by God. In the deep, deep space of aloneness, you'll speak to heaven and heaven will speak to you. The Bible will be the words through which you speak to God, and the journal will be the place of record—the record of God's words spoken to you. It will become a kind of personal Scripture that contains the questions, fears, boredom, and loneliness of your own soul, and the revelations and resolutions that come quietly to you in the silence. The Bible and your journal will become your companions and through them your desert solitude will become the canvas on which you converse with the One who loved you into being. As you near the time of your departing, commit yourself to God and even in the moment of your desire to forego the journey and stay at home, remember that even before your journey was planned, God had already prepared for you a great gift. It awaits you in the desert.

CHAPTER 3

Emptying

The air is heavy with moisture. It breathes hard and feels hard and yet, there is a gentle breeze and a relatively, mild temperature. The sun has had the curtain of cloud pulled across it and the little desert animals are grateful for the intermission. The breeze blows the pungent desert odor but today it is a wet pungency. There is no visible moisture, but the drops are simply waiting for their cue to come on stage. But, it is the heaviness that is so notable—the heaviness that breathes hard.

—from the journal of Renee Miller

They happen every year. In the deep heat of summer and early fall the clouds gather over the hot arid landscape and the thunderstorms begin. At first, there seems nothing unusual about the drum roll of thunder and the unfettering of water-drops from the sky. It's when the rain falls with quickness and intensity, as if heaven wants to rid itself of every last trace of moisture in the shortest time possible, that the flash floods threaten. A topography is designated as a desert when it receives less than ten inches of waterfall during an entire year. Yet, during the flash flood seasons, four to five inches can flow from the clouds to the ground in just a few hours. Because the earth is as dry as old crumbly chalk, it can't absorb the amount of water being dumped so relentlessly and unremittingly upon it, so it seeks a lower place. It begins to fill up the washes—the arroyos—those dry gullies that during the rest of the year are merely channels or depressions in the desert that serve as the containers for interesting rocks and litter, animal skulls and bits of driftwood. As the washes fill to overflowing with walls of water from ten to thirty feet high, what once appeared harmless becomes a devastating force to anything in its path. Plants, animals, people, and even cars can be swept along and beaten by the force of the over-filled wash. The desert arroyo must simply empty itself of what has filled it to overflowing.

Sometimes our lives are heavy like the moisture that breathes hard—heavy and in need of becoming one of those teeming washes. The daily round of roles and responsibilities can fill our every waking hour, and even find their way into the shaded dreams crossing our consciousness in the darkness of night. We become as hardened as clay fired in a kiln. Because we cannot absorb anything more, the stuff of our life begins to sink into the crevices and canyons of our soul, filling them up until even the edges become eroded. We become strangely dangerous to ourselves and others. What might have been only slight irritations in our life become messy rages. What had once been a spirit of contagious joy becomes a brooding depression. What had once been creative potential becomes flat dismal routine. The *joie de vivre* that should characterize us simply because we are human and alive becomes dull drudgery. We begin to relate differently to those around us. Our energy and enthusiasm seem stripped away and we're left stiff and frail. Finally, we come to ourselves. We realize that the erosion has become more acute than we'd imagined. As we cast about trying to identify the sources of our malaise, we become aware that we have too little empty space, too little white space in our lives. We need to be emptied so that we may reclaim the quiet beat of our centered soul.

A trendy topic these days is simplicity. There are books, songs, retreats, professional organizers, and magazines dedicated to helping us simplify our lives and our spaces. It's as if we know we need to be emptied of the clutter that fills our environment, our hearts, our souls. Yet, the more we investigate the trail of simplicity, the more it seems that we're just fingering complex threads wound like knotted yarn all through the fabric of our lives. We begin to see that simplicity applies to more than the material possessions in our lives. We become aware that our mind is filled with useless facts, unfounded worries, old hurtful memories, future plans and dreams. We begin to observe that our heart is filled with relationships, conflicted loves, unmet desires. We begin to sense that our soul is filled with doubts and fears, shame and guilt, longing and desire. We begin to recognize that there is no part of our life unaffected by complexity. From our money, to our living and working spaces, to our interior lives, we're cluttered up and yearn for the relief of being able to open a door somewhere in our life and find there an empty cupboard. Simplicity isn't a synonym for *emptiness*; it's another word for *emptying*. Rather than being a final state that we are working to achieve, simplicity is an ongoing process of emptying the cluttered debris in our lives. It's a process of learning what we can leave behind and what we can take with us on the next leg of our journey in life. The dastardly difficulty, of course, is finding the simple path when we're in the midst of the clutter.

Most us have, at one time or another, tried to clean a closet. After setting up appropriate boxes labeled "To Keep," "To Give Away," and "Not Sure," we've probably found it an almost impossible task to determine which item should go in which box. Even after successfully getting all the items into one of the boxes, we may have found ourselves going back to the "give away" box to pull out something we think we might need. In the midst of fullness, it's hard to know what to let go of in order to be less full. Imagine, on the other hand, putting every item in the closet into one box and storing it away. Several weeks later, when the memory of what's in the box has dimmed, consider sitting in front of that empty closet and deciding what to put into it, rather than what to take out of it.

Entering the desert can be like the exercise with an empty

closet. We can put all of our life there, all that we carry inside ourselves, into a box and sit in the silent vastness until we begin to gain clarity. Because the desert is empty and hasn't become so full that she can no longer extend her arms, she's free to stretch even into the furthest reaches of our soul, massaging us into a fresh feeling of wholeness. When we take the step to empty ourselves in the desert, we edge into those fearful and absolutely compelling arms and begin to see what needs to be put back into our lives.

I've always taken myself to the desert when I'm overly saturated with life. Even as a child of nine, I felt my life was too full at times. It was during my first summer in the desert, when the heat seemed to suck every trace of moisture from my body, my mouth was as dry as a rotting rubber tire, and even my skin felt scalded, that I first found the treasure of emptying myself on the desert. I took a small blanket and stepped out of the door of my grandmother's house that opened up right onto the desert. The moment I stepped on the hot sand, I became a desert wanderer. My favorite grandfather had just died, and somehow the desert felt like my empty heart. I shuffled through the sand until I was so far from the house that I was as surrounded by the desert as a small fish engulfed in the depths of the immense ocean. I searched out a tall saguaro cactus, spread out my blanket, and sat under the stately arms of that saguaro while the beams of the sun that can kill scorched my tender skin. I somehow knew then that the desert was vast enough to hold anything that was filling me up. Since that day it's never mattered to me whether it was the sizzling heat of summer, or the brisk cold of a winter's desert night. When I've had decisions to make, or life questions to answer, or wanted to divest myself of all the tawdriness that filled my life and soul, I've taken a small blanket and spread it out in the enormous sea of sand, cactus, and animals and emptied myself onto the waiting monochromatic terrain. The gracious and hospitable desert has never failed to open her arms to receive the decanting of my heart and soul, and has always left me with the gift of peace.

A Prayer Practice for Emptying: Part I

There are moments when we're under stress, or when we feel there's not enough time to complete all the tasks before us, or when we cringe when someone asks us to do yet one more thing, or when God seems as distant as Orion. These moments are an indication that our lives are overflowing. Our awareness of how full we've become is often little more than a passing thought that wafts over us like a mid-afternoon tropical cloud. It isn't until we feel breathless with our life and things begin to unravel that we realize that we need to take clear and direct action to keep from being completely overwhelmed. Before we reach that crisis point, routinely taking the pulse of our soul to see how saturated we've become will make it possible for us to realign ourselves and move toward greater balance. The first step in desert emptying isn't going to the desert, but taking a clear look at our lives with the undeniable truth of an X-ray.

To begin, find a time when you'll be uninterrupted and a place where you can concentrate with single-mindedness. Set aside thirty minutes and do the following exercise.

1. Take three or four minutes to quiet your heart and soul in the midst of God's presence by repeating the words from Isaiah 26:3: "You, Lord, give perfect peace to those who keep their purpose firm and put their trust in you" (Good News Bible).
2. Draw a circle on an empty page of your journal and fill it in with the various activities, people, roles, and responsibilities that claim your heart and attention. When you've finished, notice which things in the circle nourish your soul and keep you connected to the Holy One. Is there any empty space in the circle? What's missing from the circle? How do you think God would fill the circle?
3. Reflect and record brief answers to the following questions in your journal.

- What are the things/people in my life that find their way into my consciousness throughout the day?
- What have been the topics of my dreams in the past week?
- What are the things in my life that are so important that I'd weep if I couldn't do them?
- If I were to pour my life into an empty pail, how full would the pail be?

4. Take a few moments to thank God for the wonder of your life and for the time you've spent together.

A Prayer Practice for Emptying: Part II

Plan a time when you're free of external responsibilities and seek out a place as empty and free of disorder as possible. You might do the preliminary work of emptying a small space in your home that can become your private "desert" place. You might find a hidden and undisturbed space near a body of water, or in a forest, or on the top of a hill. You might rent a hotel room for a day, or find a simple and relatively unadorned chapel. While the place itself is not important, it does need to have minimal visual stimulation. It's the boring sameness of the desert that makes it possible to empty yourself and move toward the clarity of what needs to be reclaimed so that your soul can become again a vessel for holiness. Once the place has been selected and made ready, take a small blanket, a Bible, and your journal to your desert place. Even if you choose to sit on a chair rather than on the ground or the floor, use your blanket and let it be the symbol of your intention to be attentive to the desert experience.

Before you begin your meditation, consider Jesus' model of self-emptying. It wasn't merely for personal alignment and balance. As Scripture records, "[he] emptied himself, taking the form of a slave, being born in human likeness. And being found in human form, he humbled himself and became obedient to the point of death—even death on a cross" (Philippians 2:7–8). When Jesus took the risk to empty himself, it was so he would be filled with the purpose of heaven. While your life may be dripping with fullness that needs to be spilled out, the true reason for emptying yourself in the desert is so that you can be filled with the greater purposes of heaven. Sometimes it's difficult to determine what those purposes are because life just seems too overloaded. Sometimes it's difficult to determine what those purposes are because life feels so devoid of meaning. In either case, the process of emptying will prepare you to receive what you usually only dimly imagine.

After comfortably settling yourself in your desert place begin your emptying meditation.

1. Take a few moments to pray your heart and soul into the presence of the Holy One, by identifying and reaffirming your reasons for emptying yourself. Let those reasons wash over you like a cleansing bath that leaves you refreshed and receptive.

2. Open your eyes and give deep attention to your desert place. Note its color, its scent, its bareness, its voiceless speech, its openness and hospitality, and the presence of God that pulsates in it.

3. Open your journal and look carefully at the circle drawing that you completed in part 1, and visually offer everything in the circle to the waiting space that surrounds you.

4. In your mind's eye imagine putting the circle with everything on it into in a simple pottery container that sits in the corner of your desert place. Feel the emptiness that seeps through you after you've let go of everything on the circle.

5. With God's presence to guide you, open to a fresh page in your journal and reflect upon the following questions:

• What things would I like to have filling my consciousness throughout the day?

• What are the dreams my soul longs to dream?

• What are the things that are so important in my life that I'll weep if I'm not able to do them?

• What are the purposes of heaven that are waiting to fill me?

- Take a few moments to become aware again of the features of your desert place and thank God for the time you have spent there.

You'll find that you'll want to return to your desert place whenever you're feeling bloated with life. Always you'll find there the waiting arms ready to receive what you empty into them. Always you'll find the wisdom of God leading you to clarify what your soul most longs for. Always you'll find a simpler spirit, a quieter heart.

CHAPTER 4

Embrace

When I was a young woman in my twenties, as I was meditating one day in the desert I felt the heart of heaven say to me, "The desert will sometimes be your home." Those words epitomize for me the dynamic nature of the desert's embrace: "it holds you within its rough embrace," as I once wrote in a poem. Although the desert has been my home for most of my life, and my soul's home for almost all of it, its embrace is not enduring. Just when I'm feeling secure and serene in its arms, those arms open, and I'm not only free to leave but I feel I'm being pushed on the backside and sent away from the warmth and safety of that embrace. It's an expulsion, yet again, from the womb. A thrust from inertia to motion. A step away from the hidden darkness of being cared for into the blinding light of teeming life. A requirement to abandon safety and cling to risk. It's another experience of birth. I rebel against the propelling motion because I want to remain in the desert's wooing arms, but always the desert wins. I leave her embrace and find myself stumbling forward again into the world of pulsing life to encounter a new adventure. It's been difficult for me to accept that the role of the desert's embrace is preparation, not permanence.

It begins before we're born. We're held in the protective womb of our mother and know the fullness of being cradled in safety and peace. From the moment we're expelled against our will from that loving embrace, we seem to be forever searching for such an Eden again. When life becomes complicated and coercive, our emotions charged and volatile, our relationships tangled and intricate, the warmth of a loving embrace feels sadly elusive. It really doesn't take much anger, bitterness, missed choices, failed plans, unexpected pain, hurt, and betrayal to make our hearts feel increasingly distant from the embrace that just might dissipate our thirsty loneliness with the gentle dewdrops of simply being held in love.

The most delectable thing about being held in an embrace is that it makes it possible for us to let go. As soon as we're tenderly grasped, it is as if all that has troubled us is squeezed out of us in a deep, deep sigh. We can actually feel our body calming, our mind quieting, our soul becoming still. As we rest in those arms wrapped around us, we're surprised to hear the beat of our heart again. We're surprised to feel the muscles in our body relaxing. We're surprised that time seems to be standing still. We're surprised that we can't remember what had just been filling our mind and soul. We're surprised to be present to the moment. We're surprised to notice the easiness we feel about ourselves, about our life. We have, for the moment, let go of everything that's been weighing us down, and we're blissfully at peace in the freedom that washes over us.

While a human embrace gives us the momentary pleasure of letting go so that we can feel the peace of release, its very transitory nature always leaves us hungering for more, hungering for what will last, hungering for the comfort and safety that will keep us from having to taste the dish of slop that life can so easily deal out. It may seem like tragic news, but there's no embrace that will protect us from the seemingly random whims of life—even the embrace of the desert can't do that. I've had to learn this myself over the years.

The desert herself has much to teach us about the nature of embrace. One feels the embrace of the desert most at two times: in the midst of all-encompassing isolation, and in the deep of darkest night. Outside my condo, the desert stretches silently toward the small hills at the horizon. Often, at the break of dawn, I'll walk through the residential area until I reach the edge of the desert separated by barbed wire from the pavement of the citified street. I step over the barbed wire and begin walking through the rough terrain of moonscape rock, gravel the size of peas, and desert flora that looks as if movie producers have placed it there. In the dusk of morn that hasn't yet given way to full light, I stagger through the uneven land up a small hill and down on the other side. As I come down, I drop quickly into a valley. At the base of the valley, I see a large dry wash sporting desert debris. Larger mountains loom in the distance, and rocks and crevices surround me on every side. Stones large enough to sit on, but as uninviting as pointed boards, climb out of the desert floor trying to dissuade strangers. I perch myself half comfortably on one such stone. I sit very still as the sun begins to rise and shed her beams over the sand that's not looking forward to seeing her face yet again. I take a 360-degree scan of my surroundings and am aware that I can no longer see any human habitation, nor can my human frame be seen, even by a clever voyeur, because I've dropped down into that place of isolation where only the desert and I exist. There in the quiet of day burning away night, I'm completely embraced by the land, the animals, the sky, the sand, the silence, the sadness and hope of seclusion. The arms of the harsh environment have spread themselves out and welcomed me into them and in the thin space between death and full life, I'm awakened to the possibility of what it means to be held so deeply that I'm given the potential of becoming more than I ever thought I could be. As I settle into that embrace I learn that being held is always a more expansive experience than simply being cradled in two arms. I learn that embrace can happen without touch. I learn that the most meaningful embrace is often felt in isolation. I learn that embrace is always there, always awaiting my willingness to stop and participate. I learn that embrace creates a bond that I may later find difficult to break. I learn that embrace encourages me to let go, while it re-employs me at the same time. The embrace of God is just such an embrace, and if I would freely enter the open arms of heaven, I'd better be ready for the peace that is no peace.

Then there is the darkness. When all light has been stripped from the sky and only studded stars dot the darkened firmament, I again walk out of my tiny condo and my first awareness isn't the darkness, but the cool, dry air that passes through my nostrils making them feel like fine sandpaper. I'm frequently startled by the coolness that stands in such stark contrast to the heat generated by the sun's daytime rays. Even in the seemingly endless summer when night's temperatures are rarely below 100 degrees, there's a contrast from the brightness and scalding of the day's heat. As I begin to walk away from civilization into the darkness that has no edges, I'm keenly aware of the separation from known reality into the unknown immensity of what cannot be seen—into what is invisible. The further I walk, the more ungrounded I become. I am no longer feeling the need for boundaries around my life that make me secure but keep things unimaginative. The boundaries that make day's work unimaginative are stridently absent. The deeper I go into the desert, the darker it becomes. As my eyes begin to adjust, I'm able, through the light of the stars, to detect the shadows and shapes of the land, but there's never enough definition for me to control my environment. At the moment I come to that realization—that I have no control—I know that I'm being held in the great embrace of God's supreme wisdom. I, the unknowing one, am swallowed up into the divine arms of eternal knowing. I realize that I need no light—only faith. I need no definition—only trust. I need no boundaries—only love. As I settle into the embrace of deep dark-ness, I learn that embrace is always about relinquishing control. I learn that embrace is beyond sight. I learn that embrace involves risk. I learn that embrace will take me where I didn't want to go, and open me to things I didn't want to experience, and prepare me to return to the world of light unafraid.

A Prayer Practice for Desert Embrace:
Take a Nature Walk

The desert embrace is poignant and passionate. The embrace the desert offers is the seemingly endless emptiness that can never be filled, and when you find yourself in the midst of that desert away from all human civilization, the emptiness scoops you up and swirls you around as if you were a child being cradled and swung in the arms of a gentle, yet strong, father. But the Creator's touch stretches beyond the desert to the ocean, to the mountains, to the plains, to the forests. The embrace of the desert can be experienced in any landscape that affords isolation. Even in a topography that is close—as in a forest—all nature welcomes you into the emptiness that is beyond the mere physical elements experienced in that topography. It's good to begin your nature walk before you begin walking. On the night before your walk, spend some minutes in your bed after the darkness has overshadowed the lights of day poking around in your mind and soul. Look for the weak spots, the hungry and lonely crannies, the hurting and aching pressure points. Where are you feeling a lack of love? Where does it feel as though you've been ignored or abandoned? Where does your heart feel broken or fractured? Where does your voice feel silenced, your life meaningless, your very selfhood at risk? Don't be afraid to do a thorough scan under the watchful eye of God as you lie in your sleeping place, even if tears creep unbidden from your tightened eyes. Let truth move through you, and pray your heart's ache out to God. As you pray, let your body relax, so that your prayer can truly be released rather than gathered up again in your heart. Let it all go into the heart of God. Breathe the breath of deep release and let slumber fall upon you.

Set aside at least ninety minutes for your nature walk. Be sure that you choose a place remote and as untouched by human inter-action as possible. It would be good to plan to spend an hour in the embrace of the place you walk to, and you'll need time to walk there and back. When you arrive, find a place to sit and spend some time just taking in your surroundings. Be aware of the sounds, the colors, the shades and shadows, the energy, the beauty, the temperature, the wind, the sun. Note how you feel being there all alone. Are you frightened or do you feel as though you're finally safe? Note how it feels to be a small pebble in the midst of the mounds of stones of the natural landscape. Do you feel insignificant or do you feel as though you finally understand how you're one with everything? Note how you feel about the time that stretches before you. Do you feel anxious about how to spend it or do you feel it as a luxury you are loath to relinquish? Note how you feel about God. Do you wonder if God's presence is there with you or do you feel that presence so strongly that you believe you have finally been given a glimpse of heaven? Take some time to walk around the place you've chosen and try to sense, even identify in thought patterns, what invitation the place holds for you—what it offers you. When you sit back down, close your eyes and try to imagine the details of where you are. Then imagine that the entire space is wrapping itself around you in a gentle and tender embrace. Be attentive to such feelings as safety, clarity, peace. There in the midst of the world that God created, you are being held as carefully as the most expensive perfume inside an intricately etched urn. Stay in the "desert embrace" until you know you're ready to be discharged from it. Take some time to thank the space, and to thank God, for the love given so abundantly to you. As you walk back home, try not to think about what happened. Instead, let your heart and soul be still and revel in the lingering warmth of being held.

In the night, when you're lying in bed, take some time to reflect on your nature walk experience. Take another scan of your heart and soul and see how the empty, lonely, abandoned, and troubled spots feel now that you've felt the desert embrace. It would be simplistic to expect that all the tender or hurting parts will be healed. You're not looking so much for complete healing but the certainty that even in the midst of ambiguity, confusion, or even chaos, heaven has created spaces where you and your emotions can be held in love.

CHAPTER 5

Identity

It's the greatest task of a lifetime: coming to ourselves and understanding who we are in this world. Robert Louis Stevenson once wrote that to become what we are, and to become what we're capable of becoming, is the only end of life. The experiences of our lives, those who "people" our lives, the feelings that flow in twists and turns through the inner core of our being are some of what we are given to help us uncover the pieces of the puzzle that form the picture of who we truly are. While various feelings, experiences, people, and our own self-reflection are a part of the way we come to ourselves, we can't stop there. Because the landscape itself can be nothing other than what it is, it can be a model to help us perceive the ongoing truth of our own identity.

When I'm in the thick of life, bombarded by the daily responsibilities that make up the daily round, it's difficult to be attentive to my identity. I chug along as if nothing were more important than chugging along. The days and weeks flow into years and I lose track of who I am. It sometimes takes a crisis, or at least an awakening, to recognize that I need to take clear and swift action if I'm to reclaim my very "self." I wrote the poem "Balanced Breath" at one such point in my life:

Why have I forgotten?
Why have I forgotten,
And let my "self" get lost?
Moving within my world
At planetary speed,
Twirling, whirling, searching—
Searching for meaning
Amid the throng of
Images and work,
People and things; as if
There was nothing more than
Twirling, whirling, searching—
Searching for life's beat?
Why have I forgotten
And lost my very self?
Why have I forsaken
The path narrow and steep
That leads to the center
Of my inner being?
Why have I not gazed
Upon my own soul and
Breathed eternity?[2]

I wrote this as I realized that I was becoming less and less connected, or even aware, of my true identity. I was involved in work that was somewhat prestigious. I lived in one of the poshest and most beautiful places in the United States. I worked for someone I respected, loved, and enjoyed. I was making more money than I'd ever made. But I wasn't happy. I had no sense of fulfillment. I was becoming increasingly out of touch with who I was and what nourished and tended my soul. I felt the presence of God, but I no longer felt that "catch in the throat" that comes with living with authenticity and faithfulness to the Holy One. I'd wake in the

---

2. Renee Miller, "Balanced Breath," in *A Brief Moment of Infinite Time* (self published), 2.

middle of the night and count the hours until I'd have to return to my office. When I arrived at the office, I did my work, and I did it well. Yet, the emptiness left me feeling like a vacant echo inside a body of flesh and bones and continued to eat away every last trace of my joy and spiritual potential. I decided to resign my position and go to the desert. As expected, everyone but those closest to me were confused. They riddled me with well-meaning questions. How could I leave such an incredible job? How could I go to a barren and dry land after living in a verdant paradise? How could I give up a salary, especially when I had nothing to fall back on? How could I leave a boss and coworkers I respected and liked? Nobody understood my answers.

As radical as the decision was to step away from my secure, familiar world, I knew I'd become dwarfed where I was. I'd wandered away from the wonder of my true identity in God that is as large and expansive as the immense desert. My life had made me too small. I knew there was more, and more, and more. But if I wanted to find my large and genuine God-given self again, I had to leave what was unhealthy and go to the place that could help me discover my true identity once again. The word *identity* comes from the Latin for "the same." I'd come to a point in my life when my external world needed to be changed so that the false layers that had grown over my real identity could be peeled away. It was time for my perceived identity to come into closer union with my true identity until they were the same.

In the popular song "Horse with No Name," the band America sings, "In the desert you can't remember your name." In other words, when we step away from our known life into the desert life, we no longer remember the name that we were given, the name that others want us to have, the name we've come to understand is ours. Once we take the courageous step of letting the arms of the desert enfold us, we begin to see ourselves as if for the first time. It's like the experience of people who have undergone plastic surgery. When the bandages are removed and they look into the mirror, they no longer remember what they looked like before. They see themselves completely new. They realize they've been given another identity. The desert is a mirror through which we begin to glimpse an identity that's been with us from before we were born, but that has gotten buried under the layers of daily life. It's as if we're given a new name, a new identity, as if we're born again. And most assuredly, we're given a new task, a new path to follow. It doesn't always mean that we'll need to leave everything we know and hold dear. But it isn't possible to enter the desert landscape without serious attention and intention and leave unchanged. Our lives may just be out of balance, or we may be at the lowest place we can possibly imagine, but a journey into the desert will not leave us as we were. It's not the harshness of the desert alone. It is, rather, that there can be no masks in the desert. All the clever and artful disguises we have plastered over our tender identities are gently, but surely, removed. We stand naked and bare, as we were when first we greeted the world. This is the greatest gift of all—the nakedness. Our masks that keep us hidden from our own self can become like ill-fitting garments. They're too big or too small, too tight or too loose. We push and pull, rearrange and smooth out wrinkles in an attempt to look the way others think we should look. The desert, in its own nakedness, strips us of our poorly fitted clothes, and we wait with anticipation for clothes that are more beautifully fitted.

Jesus, like us, had been living the life handed to him. He had a name given to him at birth, he was the son of Mary and Joseph, he was an apprentice carpenter, he was a citizen of the small town of Nazareth. His future was patterned as it had been for other Jewish men like him. Then he went into the desert. Surrounded by nothing but the emptiness, silence, and isolation, he went through the struggle of dropping his known identity to claim his heavenly identity. He encountered the demons that would urge him to remain the same, to do what others did, to follow the expected patterns laid out for him. But right there in the midst of the struggle, he began to see in the mirror of the desert that his identity was larger than he had imagined. He began to catch a glimpse of the new path that he was to follow. When he had claimed his identity, he was ready to move into a future beyond his imagining.

The desert helps us perceive our identity, because the landscape is only and always the identity it has been given. Though it evolves over the centuries, the desert landscape remains what it is. The natural processes put into place by heaven itself form its identity. One such process is known as the Rain Shadow. Deserts are formed because they're located in what is called a Rain Shadow. Moist coastal winds cool as they move over mountains. The moisture of the cool air is dropped down on the coastal side in the form of rain or snow. So, when the wind passes over the mountains it's very dry and the land on the other side of the mountains is deprived of rain. When we enter the desert in order to come to ourselves, to find our identity anew, we go through our own rain shadow effect. As we move closer and closer to the desert, the moisture of our busy lives, our complicated relationships, our rigid expectations, our complex needs, our fears and anxieties—in short, all those things that hide our true identity from us—are left behind. When we enter the vast and empty space, we are empty ourselves. We come dry and dehydrated, thirsty for a new beginning, a new understanding, a new life, a new path. The desert will not fail us. When we let go of our false identity, our true identity will shine in the dry heat of desert sun.

A Prayer Practice for Recovering Identity: Part I

This practice, like others, actually begins before you go to the desert. Taking the time to reflect on the current state of your soul and mind will make you more able to recognize the identity that is revealed to you in the desert, and it will make you more ready to accept that identity. We can move so quickly into trying to right our imbalances, or "fix" the uneven edges of our lives, that we end up never really understanding why we were unbalanced and uneven in the first place, and we're easily caught unawares the next time. But, when we can give careful attention to the negative patterns within us, noting them, exploring them, trying to understand them, and where they originate, we have a much better chance of avoiding them in the future. So, set aside at least thirty minutes for this part of the prayer practice. Take a few moments to quiet yourself and attempt to be aware of the jagged and bumpy feelings within you as you try to come to a point of calm. When your breathing has slowed down and you feel centered, take some time to examine your life. You might do this by running through a typical day in your mind, or you might scan the terrain of your life as if you were looking down at it from above. The idea is to get a picture of how you are living your life, and how others experience you living your life. When you feel you have a sense of who you are in your current context, take a pen and begin to write down your reflections to the two following questions: How would you describe yourself? How would others describe you?

After making some notes, take another few minutes to try to identify the "moisture" in you that needs to be dropped to make you open to seeing the true identity that will be disclosed to you in the desert. It might be that your life is so busy that you've lost a sense of who you really are. It might be that you've so accommodated yourself to the culture by simply doing what everyone else does that you've forgotten who you really are. It might be that your relationships have become so intricate and complicated that you've given away who you really are. It might be that your needs for acceptance, security, or power have clouded your true self. It might be as simple as realizing that you have overscheduled yourself because you have been unable to say "no." Or, perhaps, you have committed yourself to so many friendships that you can't give quality time to any of them. Or, you're so interested in moving up the corporate ladder that you find you have lost the passion you had when you began your career. Try to discover all the patterns of behavior that have crept over the real you and once you have them firmly in your mind, commit them to a blank page in your journal. Before you end this part of the prayer practice, plan for a time when you can go to the "desert" for at least one hour.

A Prayer Practice for Recovering Identity: Part II

When you're ready to go to the desert, choose a place of dryness. It can be a park where there is a sandbox. If you've made yourself a desert place in your home, bring in a flat bowl filled with sand or small pebbles. As you prepare to go to the desert place, imagine a rain shadow—the water full of moisture from the sea rising and traveling toward the mountains. Envision the coolness of the air as it rises, and be aware of the over-heavy clouds that need to drop their moisture. Feel the rain, in your mind's eye, as it drops just before the wind crosses the mountains. Then picture the air pushing up over the top of the mountains. Because the heaviness has been dropped, see the clouds floating ever so lightly onto the surface below, spreading out and settling over the empty landscape.

Then imagine your own body and soul being full of the moisture of the things you identified when you did the first part of the prayer practice. Visualize letting them drop from you as you rise to go to your desert place. Try to imagine feeling as light as a feather. As you come to your desert place, try to rest easily and quietly in the dry place. Pay attention to the emptiness, the lightness, the absence of the trappings of your normal, natural, regular life. Take a few deep breaths and center yourself in the presence of the Holy One. When you feel you're in the Divine presence, read very slowly the following verses from Psalm 139:

> LORD, you have searched me out and known me; *
>   you know my sitting down and my rising up;
>   you discern my thoughts from afar.
> You trace my journeys and my resting places *
>   and are acquainted with all my ways.
> Indeed, there is not a word on my lips, *
>   but you, O LORD, know it altogether.
> Where can I go then from your Spirit? *
>   where can I flee from your presence?
> For you yourself created my inmost parts; *

you knit me together in my mother's womb.
I will thank you because I am marvelously made; *
My body was not hidden from you, *
> *while I was being made in secret*
> *and woven in the depths of the earth.*

Your eyes beheld my limbs, yet unfinished in the womb;
all of them were written in your book; *
> *they were fashioned day by day,*
> *when as yet there was none of them.*

Search me out, O God, and know my heart; *
> *try me and know my restless thoughts.*

As you read, let the words seep into you like the coolest water on the hottest day. Feel how they refresh each cell, each sinew, each bone, each muscle, each breath. After you have finished reading, reflect on the following questions:

1. What do you think the Holy One had in mind when you were created?
2. When was the last time that you felt your understanding of yourself and God's understanding were nearly the same?
3. If you were to stand before the Holy One right now, what would the Holy One tell you about yourself?
4. If you were to accept your true identity, what in your life would need to change?

After reflecting and writing some notes about your reflections in your journal, take five minutes to be immersed in the great desert space and see if the Holy One has any further word for you. Before leaving your desert place, touch the sand or pebbles and thank the Holy One for the time that you have spent together.

CHAPTER 6

Darkness

Desert darkness is a time to enter into silence deeper than the mere absence of words and sit quietly and still in that silence until a word forms in the soul. The darkness is the cradling companion, not the enigmatic enemy.

—from the journal of Renee Miller

I remember the black horror I felt after the terrorist attacks on September 11, 2001. I was living in the desert at the time, and it seemed that the only way to deal with my own inability to make sense of the events was to walk in the darkness each night. There's a unique quality about darkness in the desert. Not only is it so vast that your eye can't take it in, it hangs deep: it hovers like a great umbrella with panels that droop from the height of heaven to the dust of earth. Hanging just as deep, the stars too numerous to count shine like the purest diamonds. It's as if in the middle of the dark womb where nothing at all can be detected or defined, the diamonds are reminders that nothing can ever be lost. I needed to be reminded of that just then. So I'd step outside and walk toward the desert darkness until there was nothing but the darkness and me. As large and quiet as the desert darkness is, I was astonished by a unique absence of noise. I wrote in my journal on September 14,

2001: "For two nights now, there have been no planes in the sky and the star-studded blackness has felt to me more eternal, more vast, more holy. Since the awful events of September 11, it is the night-time sky that has seemed so much more silent than the daytime sky. There is a kind of hush over the world as it grieves. . . ." I came to an important realization about the desert on those nightly strolls. What had been just the other side of daytime for me now became the womb of protection and the harbinger of hope. It would be the darkness itself that would heal and restore.

It was there at the beginning of creation. It was "the stuff" from which creation came. "In the beginning when God created the heavens and the earth, the earth was a formless void and darkness covered the face of the deep. . . . Then God said, 'let there be light'; and there was light" (Genesis 1:1–3). Everything that we know, cherish, and delight in was born out of the primal darkness. From the trees, to our children, to the choice of our particular career, to the memories that are scratched on the surface of our souls, to the experience of God in the silent part of our being—all of it was conceived and grew in the darkness before ever it was birthed in the light. It's as if darkness is the endless ocean through which light must sail. Without the darkness, there would be no possibility of sailing; in fact, there'd be no movement whatsoever. Whenever we can detect the periphery—the edges—of light, we see that just beyond those edges is the great deep darkness that stretches into eternity. There is no escape from that darkness. Nor should there be.

There is, within the human psyche, it seems, an innate distrust of the darkness. We tend to prefer a light, sunny day to a dark, moon-less night. The darkness seems to conjure up fears in us that can so easily be set aside during the day. From childhood, we're cautioned about going out alone at night and taught that darkness is the place where evil lurks. We're programmed to strain for the light to avoid the invisible and often seductive temptations that creep out of dark-ness trying to snatch unsuspecting victims. Over time, we become unaccustomed to finding our way in the dark. We try to tell ourselves that it isn't logical to be so afraid, since we know that our lives are not quantitatively or qualitatively different just because the sun has set and night has come on. We know that both the darkness and the light are really part of one complete movement. There really is no difference between the night and the day. Yet, we rarely choose to take our "power walk" in the deep of night, or keep the lights off in our home when the sun's rays have fled the sky. We've all probably had the experience of waking up in the night finding ourselves worried or fearful. What worries us or causes us fear is so real it can make our heart thump so hard that it feels like a brick trying to escape from inside the walls of our chest. Adrenalin courses through our veins and quickens our pulse. The images swirling around in our mind amplify the longer we lie there. But when the shades of light make their way through the darkness and we wipe the sleep from our eyes, everything seems to have been put back into place. What was so fearsome in night's shadows has no potency in sun's light.

The ambiguity we feel about the darkness hovering over us like a cool, hazy cloud spills over into the very fabric of our daily lives. We become as terrified of darkness in our life and relationships as we are of the physical blackness of night. We find ourselves attempting to avoid any possibility of being plunged into the deep cavern of life's darkness lest we find ourselves unable to breathe, unable to reach for help, unable to find meaning, unable to express love, unable to halt a loneliness that cuts like a dull knife through the tender tendrils that surround our soul. But the loss of our job, or a death of someone we love, or the revelation that our child is addicted to drugs, or the news of an impending national crisis, or the announcement by our doctor that we have a terminal illness, or the complete disintegration of our financial future can make us feel we've been cut in strips and abandoned on a road to fend for ourselves without the resources to bring us back to full life. When we're in the throes of these struggles, all we want is to escape. We want to go to the desert—not a physical desert necessarily, but a vacant and silent landscape where we can lament and whine, scream and grieve. We want to go where no one will hear us but the landscape. Where no one will try to tell us our troubles aren't so bad. Where no one will tell us to "get over it and get a life." Where no one will minimize or diminish our feelings of despair. We want to unleash our pain and let it reverberate off the rocks and sand, to pour out our salty tears until puddles form and we are completely drained of the everlasting ache that bullies us and seems never to abate.

But the darkness does abate. The shades of color change and we change, too. Surprisingly, after time has passed and the silhouettes of light have emerged on our personal horizon, we look back and find that in the midst of what had been so horrific, the gift of grace was there, sitting as still as a well-behaved child. Even there in the pit from which we thought there was no reprieve, the Spirit of God was standing over us. The very troubles that seemed so difficult, the very things we would never have wanted to be exposed to, the very things we would not have chosen for ourselves actually become a means of life and blessing for us.

When we escape to the desert to break away from the darkness of our lives, we find that the darkness we bring along with us can never equal the deep and cavernous darkness that awaits us there in the isolated, sandy landscape. At first, the desert darkness feels like a threatening and overpowering force that will swallow us up without leaving even the faintest trace of our presence on this earth. But the longer we sit in the desert darkness, the more familiar it becomes and the more secure we become. We begin to see it as a prevailing condition of life. We come to understand and value the truth that everything that is born begins in darkness. When we leave the desert, the darkness of our own lives is not inevitably lifted from us, but we no longer feel the need to run away from it or surround ourselves with false light in order to deny its presence. We're mysteriously able to let the darkness wash over us, while we wait in silent patience for the light of new life to peek through. When the darkness of terror was unleashed on September 11, I felt as if I was adrift and unable to make sense of even the smallest details of life. By taking myself into the physical darkness as a kind of spiritual practice, I began to see the threads of hope and life that the darkness held. I no longer needed to feel paralyzed. I could let the physical darkness wrap around me and hold me until I was able to see a new light.

A Prayer Practice for Desert Darkness: Part I: The Physical Darkness

Begin this practice by plotting out a place and time to be present in a space of deep darkness. Since the sky becomes ebony all over the globe, you don't have to be in the physical desert to experience the darkness. Just choose a place where the sky is big and where competing lights are minimal. Choose an area that is as unpopulated as possible—perhaps around a lake, at the side of the ocean, in a park, or in your own backyard. If there's no opportunity to experience the largeness of the sky because you live in an urban area or a forest, you can choose to go to your "desert place" in your home. If you opt for your desert place, you'll find that the darkness feels more confining because there is nothing beyond the ceiling, and there are no diamonds pricking the darkness with flickers. You will be able to increase the breadth of the darkness by making sure that it is truly dark. Turn out the lights in any rooms that are in close proximity to your desert place. Throw blankets over the windows if you find lights from the street shining in. Try to make your space so dark that you can't even see your hand in front of you.

Before you actually enter the space, read the experience of Saul who, after encountering the heart of heaven, found his sight taken from him for three days and nights:

Now as [Saul] was going along and approaching Damascus, suddenly a light from heaven flashed around him. He fell to the ground and heard a voice saying to him, "Saul, Saul, why do you persecute me?" He asked, "Who are you, Lord?" The reply came, "I am Jesus, whom you are persecuting. But get up and enter the city, and you will be told what you are to do." The men who were traveling with him stood speechless because they heard the voice but saw no one. Saul got up from the ground, and though his eyes were open, he could see nothing; so they led him by the hand and brought him into Damascus. For three days he was without sight. (Acts 9:3–9a)

After you've settled yourself in the darkness and become accustomed to it, focus your thoughts on your breath. Breathe in a measured and unhurried way until you feel that your heartbeat has slowed. Take a few moments to feel the immensity of the darkness around you and the presence of the Holy One in the midst of that darkness. Then, reflect on the following questions: What must it have been like for Saul to be thrust against his will into a darkness from which there was no escape? When has the darkness in my life been so great that I felt I could no longer see? When has the darkness in my life led me to the light?

After spending several minutes meditating on the questions, bring your attention once again to the darkness surrounding you, to your rhythmic breathing, to the regular beat of your heart, and the silent presence of the Holy One. Allow the darkness to wrap itself around you like a gentle cloak and let yourself drop down, down, down into it, as if you were being lowered into a deep dark well. When you feel fully encompassed within the blackness, offer a prayer to the Holy One in thanksgiving for the time you have spent together.

Part II: The Interior Darkness

We can find it particularly frightening to encounter the darkness that exists within our own being. We're so used to having answers, solving problems, and responding to crises that the idea of tunneling inward to find grace, in the darkness, is not only foreign but frightful. But it's only when we freely enter into the darkness that we can detect the light. This practice of tunneling inward can bring us to a new awareness of the importance of the darkness to deepen our lives and make them more real, more full, more whole. Set aside at least thirty minutes. Take a journal and pen and go to your desert place or a place where you'll be undisturbed and where you can feel a sense of peace. Then, begin the simple process of traveling into your own deep dark and wondrous life.

- Take five minutes to quiet yourself
- Imagine that you're walking through a desert expanse and come to a small mountain. You notice that there is a small cleft carved out in the mountain and you focus your attention on climbing into that small cleft. Once there you find it's really a tiny cave. You make your way into the back part of the cave and sit on a flattened rock with your back against the wall. You feel shielded and protected from the world outside the cave. The darkness of the place cradles you in silence and safety. After a few moments you realize that you're not alone. Your heart quickens, but then quiets again as soon as you realize it's the Holy One who is there with you. After acknowledging and greeting the One who has loved you from before time, you ask for the grace to see clearly what the Holy One already knows about you.
- Take out your journal and write from the depth that you can only believe is there within you. To get the thoughts flowing, begin by completing the following:

The great treasure that is buried within me that I had forgotten is . . .

- Write until you sense a light beginning to flicker within you and within the darkness of the cave. As the light grows, let your mind detach from the darkness and imagine walking out of the desert into the broad light of mid-day.

As you greet the first shades of light, offer a prayer of intention to return often to the darkness of the cleft rock, where the radiance of God can illumine your soul.

CHAPTER 7

From Silence to Sound

We come to the desert anxious for a cessation of sound. We're weary of the noise that's infected our every waking moment, leaving us feeling like our bodies have become little more than conductors of clamor and clatter. From the swish of the agitating washing machine, to the plaintive cry of our child's weeping, from the shrillness of irritating sirens, to the hum of yet one more opinion in an already boring meeting, we find our souls have become serrated on the edges by the neverending necessity of sound. Yet as eager as we are to step away from sound so that our soul's frayed edges might be melded back together again, we soon think that the cacophony of our busy life is preferable to the overpowering desert silence. It's not long after being dropped down into the silence that we begin to find ourselves babbling. Even if our mouths are silent, our hearts jibber and jabber just to punctuate the monotony of the vacant quiet. Abba Poemen, one of the early Desert Fathers, understood this: "Someone may seem to be silent, but if in the heart one is condemning others, then one is babbling ceaselessly. And there may be another who talks from morning to evening, and yet in the heart that person is truly silent."[3]

---

3. John Chryssavgis, *In the Heart of the Desert* (Bloomington, Ind.: World Wisdom, Inc., 2003), 45.

The trouble isn't that there's an absence of sound in the desert, but the sound in that desolate and empty place is so different than it is in our workaday world. The sound conforms more closely to the actual meaning of the word *sound* than it does to our practical experience of sound. Sound is nothing more than vibrations transmitted through a liquid, a gas, or even an elastic solid—a solid that is bendable and flexible. In our practical experience these vibrations draw together to form words that have become our familiar and recognizable friends. We are rarely aware of the singular and random vibrations that stand solitary before they're connected to the other vibrations that eventually become decipherable sounds. Because we're so accustomed to interpreting what sounds mean rather than how they're formed, we don't listen as closely as we might as the solitary vibrations slither through liquid, as they shoot through gas, as they twist and weave through solids that are flexible. "How can a solid be flexible?" we may find ourselves asking. It's difficult to conceive that a solid mass of matter is really pure energy moving at a speed faster than the eye can catch, and that it can actually bend and curve even though it appears to be immoveable. Because this is difficult to conceive, we can find ourselves so content with what is before us that we don't take the time for the deeper listening and deeper watching that can take us to new places of experience and understanding.

There's much that is moving in the desert even though from a distance it seems as dead and calcified as old bones uncovered in a darkened tomb. Even what doesn't seem to be moving is curving to the cadence of nature's rhythm and sound is being produced, though it doesn't necessarily result in distinguishable words. Desert tones have to be listened to through the random isolated vibrations that begin in lone-ness and then bond with other vibrations to form sound. In other words, desert sound is discovered through desert silence. Desert sound is discovered while the vibrations still stand solitary.

An alternative definition of sound is perhaps even more poignant, as it applies to the sounds of the desert: "sound is the distance over which something can be heard."[4] Noise, in order to be heard, actually needs space—empty space—through which the vibrations that make up sound can travel. Because the desert is such a vast space of emptiness, tones ought to be shaped even more intensely there, and yet those tones are still so hard to detect. Again, the problem is not located in the absence of sound. Rather, we are simply too unfamiliar with the kind of listening required in the desert. To hear what we long to hear, we need to develop a different style of listening, so that we can identify the sound that is most assuredly present in that bare and broad expanse.

The rattler, one of the most fearsome of all snakes, is a good example of desert sound. Unlike so many other desert animals and wildlife that scratch the sand with their claws, creating sound wherever they go, the rattler makes no such sound when moving. Like all snakes, it slides silently as it moves forward. However, the rattlesnake is an interesting mixture of silence and sound. While it slinks so silently along the rocks and dry fissures of the desert landscape, it can also produce a warning sound to predators by shaking its rattles. It's content to live in silence, only shaking its rattles when provoked, frightened, or at risk. It hibernates all winter, but by early spring it's awake and searching for warm sunny rocks to spend a languorous afternoon. When the heat of summer begins to descend, it adopts a secretive and stealthy posture, doing most of its hunting at night, and trying to stay out of the scalding heat of day. If we're inattentive, we won't notice that a rattlesnake is nearby, but if it shakes its rattles, the intense and haunting sound will reverberate within us forever. In this dangerous snake, the curious interplay of silence and sound teaches us the importance of concentrated listening in the desert if we are to hear the external sounds that leer menacingly and the internal sounds that are all but drowned out by the busyness of our lives. Because the desert silence is so big, it would seem that the sounds there would be

---

4. *The American Heritage Dictionary of the English Language, Fourth Edition* (Boston: Houghton Mifflin, 2000, 2004).

strong and unmistakable, because they are in such contrast to the silence. Yet, without determined eavesdropping, we can be so overwhelmed by the silence that we're deaf to the very sound that has the potential of transforming us—the whisper of the voice of the Holy One.

When we come to the desert, we feel ready to hear the sound of God's voice, eager to have our ears pierced by the loving tones of heaven's melody. We come expectant, certain that it will be easier to detect the voice of God in the place of sheer silence. If we can detach from all the words, images, roles, and responsibilities that are so common to our everyday lives, we feel confident that in a place without those words, images, roles, and responsibilities we will not miss the movement of God's Spirit in us. But, like the great prophet Elijah, we can find that when we get into the desert wilderness, the voice of God seems strangely elusive. We expect to encounter God in the fiery heat, or in the shaking of the earth, or in the passionate storms, but it can feel like the Holy One is absent from the expected meeting places. Then, when we're beginning to feel disillusioned, and the silence has become more than the quiet of the landscape, and we've concluded that God is nowhere to be found, we begin to listen to the silence in a way that we hadn't before. We start to develop that style of listening that the desert requires. Divine music begins to form over the vast emptiness of space and a wisp of tone begins to take shape around us, and we hear the still, small voice of God. In the instant that we listen across the emptiness, we are aware of how immense the silence really is and how the murmur of heaven is more like a comma than an exclamation point. The troubles we brought with us to the desert seem to be ladled up into the wideness of God's mercy and we no longer need to fill the silence with our own words, or try to coyly coerce God to speak with us.

St. Antony, the father of desert monasticism, found this to be true in his own life. Although Antony struggled for some time with demons within and without,

The Lord was not forgetful of Antony's struggle. God was at hand to assist him. So, looking up, Antony saw the roof, as it were, opened, and a ray of light descended upon him. The demons suddenly vanished, the pain of his body immediately ceased, and the building was calm again. Conscious of this grace, Antony regained his breath and felt free from pain. He spoke to the vision that appeared to him, saying, "Lord, where were you? Why did you not appear at the beginning in order for me not to endure such pain?" And a voice came to Antony, saying, "Antony, I was here all the time; I simply waited to witness your fight. Now, since you have endured, and not yielded, I shall be your assistance forever, and I shall make your name known everywhere." Having heard this, Antony rose up and prayed, receiving such strength that he perceived that he had never had more power in his body previously.[5]

The desert offers us the silence that is deeper than our hearts can imagine and the soft sigh of the Holy One who brings the words of life. But that sigh comes only to those who have exhausted every expectation of what it means to encounter that Holy One and are prepared to listen with the soul to the solitary vibrations that come from heaven itself.

A Prayer Practice for Moving from Silence to Sound

It always feels like a miraculous experience when the sound of God breaks through the deep silence of our lives, when we're deeply aware of the sound and able to distinguish its origin. Consider the ancient story of Adam and Eve in the Garden of Eden. After they'd tasted the fruit of unhealthiness, they suddenly realized that they were naked and they covered themselves with fig leaves. They had a newfound understanding about themselves and about the Holy One. Instead of feeling as secure as children at the park with their parents on Sunday afternoon, they felt exposed and vulnerable.

---

5. Ibid., 104.

They now knew something about their own frailty, and the silence of too much self-knowledge had settled upon them. Then they heard the voice of God walking in the garden in the cool of the day, and they hid themselves from God's presence. They heard the voice—the sound—of God walking. Hearing pure spirit moving through the cool evening breeze was a sound unlike any other. It was a sound that was unmistakable and undeniable. Neither the silence that had settled over them, nor the silence that settles over us is ever permanent or final. The presence and word of the Holy One can break through the most colossal silence in our environment and in our souls. Hearing the sound of the Holy One walking in the wind requires a deep and profound listening that is occasioned by acute awareness. This prayer practice will help develop the ability to exercise such awareness.

Begin this process by choosing an outdoor place as free of distraction as possible—perhaps an open field, or a tree-lined park, or a secluded place along the water's edge. Take a journal and pen with you and try to schedule the practice for a time during the early evening, just as the day is ready to step aside so the night can begin its journey toward birth once again.

- After you've found a sitting place and settled into it, begin to take in your surroundings. Jot down in your journal what you notice as you look around. Do you feel private and secluded? Is the sky particularly wide? How does the water dance? Are there clouds skirting across the sky? Is the air warm and full? Try to capture in words or images the characteristics of the environment.
- Begin to notice what's going on inside your soul. Again, jot down in your journal a description of the state of your soul at this moment using words or images. Are you feeling fearful? Where are you feeling exposure or vulnerability in your life? Do you have any anxiety about hearing the voice of the Holy One? What are the unhealthy patterns of your life that are obstacles between you and the Holy One?
- Now that you have scanned the external world and your internal

soul, set your journal aside and close your eyes. Allow the silence, which may be interspersed at times by the sounds of nature, to wash over you. Sit in the silence for at least ten to fifteen minutes. Allow the silence to wrap around you without hindering it. When you find yourself longing for speech, or at least for something else to be happening, repeat the phrase, "This is God's earthly temple—let silence be the sign of my openness to God." Return to the phrase whenever you feel you are uneasy or fidgety.

• Offer a prayer inviting the Holy One to speak to you through the silence. Take a few moments to pay keen attention to the slightest movement of air around you. The air may appear to be quite still, but with awareness you may notice that there is a slight breeze flowing through the space. Feel it brush your skin, move through your hair, become one with the breath in your nostrils. Notice the slenderness of sound as the air moves. It may seem to be devoid of all noise, but with more focused attention, you will actually hear its movement.

• Let your soul be bathed in the sound, and observe what images begin to form in your heart, what words seem to flash across the canvas of your mind, what feelings seem to be bubbling up within you. You may not hear God's voice in words that you are accustomed to hearing, because the sound will come from the connection of solitary vibrations, but the sound of God's voice can be discerned in those solitary vibrations that show up in images, interior feelings, and random thought patterns. Let the sound of these vibrations stream through you until everything returns to silence again.

Record in your journal the sound of God's voice that you heard and how you think you will respond. Then thank God for the miracle of communion, the wonder of relationship, the marvel of the meeting of heaven and earth.

CHAPTER 8

From Solitude to Holy Company

The solitude that has called us, wooed us, allured us in its vast embrace will always offer us more than the escape we thought we came to enjoy. When our life seems so full that it looks like an overflowing cart and we feel like we can't move forward without unbalancing the cart and finding the contents spilled all over the ground, the idea of being completely and totally alone is seductively attractive. The possibility of being free from all responsibilities and voices that are trying to manage and manipulate our time and energy feels like a fresh bloom in the midst of deep winter. The broad expanse stands before us like the greatest freedom. We have little comprehension of the demands such solitude will require and little notion of the hard grace that we will encounter there. We do not imagine that we will face the demons of loneliness and boredom and engage in a fierce struggle with them. We don't know we'll be exposed to the reality of our own selves, without benefit of defense, justification, rationalization, or even averred ignorance. It never occurs to us that our heart will undergo the flame of fire searing it until it is pure. In short, we don't realize that there's a greater purpose to the solitude than escape from an over-full, unbalanced life.

The rough grace that the desert provides is found most palpably in the heat so characteristic of desert topographies. From the time we were children taking geography class in elementary school, we've known that the summer heat in the deserts of the world can be brutal. This intense heat is generated because there is so little moisture in the air. When the moisture barrier in the atmosphere is so thin, most of the sun's energy reaches the surface, unleashing on the sandy, rocky earth the heat that can kill—and heal. As the sand absorbs the extreme heat of the sun, it becomes a conductor of radiant heat, releasing it into the air. It's this vicious heat that singes and blisters the skin, sucks water and air from every cell of the body, and leaves the skin crackled like a lizard's back. Heat can obviously be dangerously destructive, but it also has the potential of burning away impurity until only the true beauty of a thing is left, shining like a diamond in a darkened cave. The heat of the desert lives up to this potential if we're open to it. It burns away every pretense and sham from the fabric of our heart, leaving it so pure that it can see God. And, once we begin to see God, we have a greater possibility of developing a deeper union with that God. In the language of heat, this would be called "thermal equilibrium." When the heat in one substance is put in contact with the cold of another substance, they both eventually become warm. Because heat always moves toward cold, that heat flows into the cold substance until there is a balance—until the two have reached the same temperature. Just as this occurs in the landscape, so it occurs in our heart. The burning heat of God's love flows into the coldness of our heart until there's a balance between the two—until the two reach the same temperature—until there is a union between the two. The greater purpose of the solitude of the desert is to allow us to move closer to that divine union.

When we think we're evading the imbalance of our life by going into desert solitude, we're surprised to find that it is wasn't merely our own desire for relief that led us there. It was the Holy One stirring up the desire in our heart because the Holy One wants to meet us there, where there are no competing voices, tasks, or false loves. Hosea the prophet understood this when the words of God came to him: "I will now allure her, and bring her into the wilderness, and speak tenderly to her" (Hosea 2:14). The greater purpose of the solitude of the desert is to engage us in an encounter with the Holy One—an encounter that will change us forever. Little do we know, when we're feeling overloaded with life and longing to go off and be alone, that we're really longing not for solitude, but for God. In the cacophony of our daily lives, we feel God is hiding, and the deep river of longing that courses through the cut channels of our being is hungry not for freedom but for God. We may feel a sense of belonging in our families and communities, we may feel a sense of belonging in our work and in the geography in which we reside, but the deep existential belonging for which our soul yearns feels swallowed up by the lives we lead. We've actually come to experience, though we may not be able to adequately articulate it, an absence of belonging. We come to the desert not for separation, but for closeness—the feeling of being intimate and belonging together with the Holy One.

When we first encounter the desert solitude, we're enveloped by the sheer wonder of being alone and unaccountable to anyone for anything. It feels as delicious as a juicy strawberry dripping with dark chocolate. We want to lick the chocolate off slowly, savoring its bittersweet taste, then nibble the strawberry still redolent with chocolate flavor. But after a time, the delightful strawberry is gone, and we feel loneliness and boredom seeping in and we begin to feel stripped and raw. The desert now seems to be no help at all; it seems to have become a cruel companion intent on banishing us from everything and everyone that makes it possible for us to hide from the reality of our own being. We want nothing more than to leave and return to the filmy existence that keeps such reality at bay. When we've reached that point when fleeing the desert seems as attractive, indeed imperative, as fleeing our lives to go to the desert once was, we feel a curious warmth around us and we're suddenly aware that we are not alone.

I had gone on a private desert retreat because it was something I thought was good for me to do every year, I hoped to deepen my spiritual life, I was anxious to get away from people, and because

I wanted to show others that I had the courage to go on a long, silent retreat in an arid desert setting in the heat of summer. It was a quiet and nearly deserted retreat center—not many participants during the summer months. I arrived with my few belongings: my clothes, my Bible, a book of prayer, a journal, and pen. I didn't take chocolate-covered strawberries, but I brought a dozen homemade chocolate chip cookies. A desert veteran, I knew the time would come when I'd want to avoid the loneliness and boredom. The cookies would give me a reprieve and a small modicum of comfort. The first couple of days were sheer luxury. No phone, no bills, no work. Plenty of languorous sleep, waking to the woeful and haunting tune of mourning doves, eating simple and healthy food, watching surreal sunsets, and knowing the blessedness of autonomy and liberation.

But the time came, as it always does in the desert, when loneliness loomed and boredom burned and the cookies were all gone. When I thought I couldn't tolerate one more day in that God-forsaken, scorching, hot, empty wasteland, I felt the heat that is stronger even than the sun—the heat of God's love. "Ah," my soul whimpered. It came quietly and I knew it at first as tenderness. I was solitary and isolated but I was no longer alone. The hours would no longer stretch across my being with nothing but fear, anguish, and despair. I'd entered the space of divine love and the heat was warming my cold heart and bringing me into closer union with the Holy One. I could easily have basked the rest of the retreat in the sweetness of that love, but, as I've said before, the desert is the place of preparation, a training ground for something else. Its comfort is a sacred dis-ease, its peace a sacred disturbance.

In some ways it would be easier if the encounter with the Holy One remained hierarchical. But the Holy One is never content with building structure and exercising authority. Rather, it is a connective relationship, one that leaves no masks, no unturned stones, no possibility for easy dismissal. It's the fostering of this connective relationship that's at the core of the encounter. So, I knew there would be no basking in a sentimental and saccharine tenderness.

The heat of God's love was meant to transform and prepare me for a return to my world. The last days of the retreat were filled with gratitude for the holy company that is wonder-full and fierce: holy company that won't let us off the hook but surrounds us with grace and strength as limitless as the desert itself. It's this alone that makes it possible not only to take up the daily life again, but to live that life from the balance forged in the burning fire of divine desert Love.

A Prayer Practice for Moving from Solitude to Holy Company

This prayer practice is more demanding because it requires going into solitude long enough to have the time to struggle with the inner demons that are normally hidden by our busy lives. It's important to experience the nefarious nature of these demons, because as long as we keep them hidden it's difficult to feel the presence of the rugged grace that stands so close and yet is so eagerly avoided. Experiencing the Holy One's breath nearby is often only noticed when our illusions, our comforts, our security blankets have been taken away from us. When we're laid bare, and our soul stands as naked as a stripped tree in winter, we feel the breath of the Holy One with absolute certainty.

When you begin this practice, clear a weekend or a week from your calendar. If you've never been on a silent, private retreat, a weekend will be enough. If you're accustomed to longer retreats, then schedule at least a week. If you can, you might choose to make reservations at a retreat house in one of the Southwest desert regions. If not, find a place near your home where you can be in solitude. You might choose a retreat center in your town, in the home of an out-of-town friend, or in an inexpensive hotel room. Make your reservations well in advance, so that your heart can have time to prepare for the experience.

Before the retreat, take a few moments every day to visualize being alone without your cherished belongings and possessions, without your normal modes of communication like your cell phone and computer, without the tenderness or friction of the people in your life, without any conversation whatever. After visualizing and feeling this as deeply as you can, consider in your soul why you're going on this retreat: You're going away from everything you know in order to become closer with the One who alone knows you. Remember that while you're trying to prepare yourself, God is also at work preparing your heart for the time you'll spend together. Try to imagine being in your place of solitude with no one but God. Visualize and feel the immense gift of the encounter that awaits you.

When it's time to go on the retreat, be parsimonious in what you lug along with you. It will be enough to take a few clothes, a Bible, a journal, a candle or incense—and maybe some chocolate chip cookies. When you arrive at your place of solitude and you've closed the door behind you, stand very still and offer yourself to the space and to God who shares the space with you. Breathe in the emptiness, breathe out your fullness. Feel the breath in you becoming slower and deeper as your body begins to relax muscle by muscle. There are no rules for your retreat time, but a few guidelines might help.

1. Each day spend time when you awake, at mid-morning, right after lunch, before dinner, and before bed to read a portion of Scripture and meditate on it using the following process:

   • Take a few moments to center yourself by taking some deep breaths and affirming the presence of God in your midst.
   • Slowly read the passage completely.
   • Re-read it thought by thought, very slowly. Ask God to speak to you about the thought and what your response to it should be. Do not move on to the next thought until you feel you have reached some clarity.
   • After going through the entire passage in this way, offer a short prayer of thanksgiving.

- Jot down in your journal any thoughts, insights, or questions that came to you during the prayer time.

2. Eat simple and healthy food. Don't overeat because it will make it difficult for you to be fully attentive during the prayer periods.
3. Take a long walk at least once each day.
4. Throughout the time of the retreat try to be aware of the following and record your experiences in your journal:

   - times when your heart feels warmed
   - times when your heart feels disturbed
   - the moment when you realize you are no longer alone
   - the ways that you are being prepared to return to your daily life again

5. When you begin to encounter the demons within you, and your cookies are all gone, you'll find yourself wanting to "phone home," or cut the retreat short and return home early, or eat, or to sleep more than you know you should. When any of these feelings wash over you and you're certain you won't be able to last another moment, any of the following may help:

   - Sit very quietly and pay attention to your breathing until you feel the crisis pass.
   - Pretend that you won't leave the room alive and write down your feelings in your journal.
   - Take a short walk.
   - Do some stretching exercises.

As soon as you've tried one of these and you feel a bit more settled, immediately sit down and drop your eyes into your soul and try to read what's going on there, and ask God to help you identify why you're having these feelings. Reaffirm that you've come here simply to be completely alone with God—to enter into a deeper union with the Holy One. The way to move from fear and frustration is to abandon yourself into the very space you want to flee, because it's in that space that you'll find your own true self, and it's there that the fierce company of the Holy One will prepare you to live from that true self. Trust that and relinquish yourself into the embrace of God.

CHAPTER 9

From Emptying to Emptiness

We'd decided that a small trip into the open desert would be an adventure. My husband, son, foster son, and I packed a few supplies and plenty of water into backpacks and drove to a place where we could park the car and begin a trek into the virgin desolate landscape. We left the car around mid-afternoon and started hiking until we were completely out of sight and out of range of human contact. The desert stretched endlessly before us and we trudged along, feeling the warmth of the spring sun, delighting in the blooming cacti and desert wildflowers that, for a short while during springtime, turn the dull monotonous color scheme of the desert into a gentle yet lively playground of rich color. We were on our guard for rattlesnakes that, like us, were anxious to enjoy such an extraordinarily beautiful spring day. The only sounds were those that the desert makes. Though we were only a few miles from civilization, we might have been at the end of the earth for the isolation we experienced. Before evening had brushed across the sand, we wanted to reach a small mountain ahead in hopes of finding a cave where we could take shelter for the night. While none of us had any experience or desire for spelunking (we actually didn't even like camping!), we knew it would be safer to sleep in a cave than to plop ourselves down on the rocky sand where we would have no protection from wild boars and roaming cattle, sliding snakes and surly scorpions, skulking coyotes and menacing humans. It took us only a short climb up the mountain to find a suitable cave and with a small bit of daylight left we were able to scout around inside the cave to be sure it was relatively free of desert creatures. We laid out our sleeping bags and prepared for a pleasant slumber. It's so often true that what feels so safe in daylight is filled with uneasiness in the ebony of night. Unaccustomed to the screeching sounds of the nighttime desert, the night, for me, was anything but pleasant. The cocoon of darkness inside the cave was meant to be protective, but without the benefit of even the light of the stars, every sound was magnified, every shadow surreal. My imagination became larger than life and fears that would have seemed ridiculous in daylight seemed to plunder every cell of my body. It felt like even eerie echoes of desert spirits would insure that my sleep would be disturbed. Needless to say, it was a long, long night, and when the sun began to push away the black darkness, the tension in my body finally eased and I felt like I had been given back my life. I had no desire, on that trip, to stay another night in that sinister hole just beyond the zone of light. I was ready for a soft, cozy room at a luxury hotel, with lights that could keep the darkness of night, and the darkness of my soul, under control.

Over the years, I've learned that the only way to overcome the fearsomeness of a desert cave is not to leave it too quickly. We're easily urged to abandon a cave after one miserably unsettling night, and when we do, we miss what the cave has to offer us. The early Desert Fathers never tired of telling their disciples to stay in their cell, because their cell would teach them everything. A *cell* is but another word for *cave*. Those holy desert dwellers didn't live in well-designed, modern-day monasteries that house monks in cells that are small bare rooms outfitted with a bed, a chair, and a desk. Most of them lived in caves just like the one I found so distasteful. Their cave was their cell, and in it, they struggled with their own selves—their fears, their overactive imaginations, their temptations, their doubts, their lack of trust in God's presence. They were surrounded with a deeper darkness than the darkness of a room without lights. They had to face the darkness of their own illusions and tunnel yet deeper into the blackness until they found the light of God. Naturally, there were times when they wanted nothing more than to flee the cave, but only by remaining in the cave did they find inner peace.

At first, a desert cave or cell feels fearful because it is unfamiliar. The unusual scents and strange sounds, and being unable to see clearly, make it feel terrifying rather than shielding. The cave appears to be as confining as a prison. We begin to recognize that all of our usual capers to keep the unknown from encroaching too close upon us will not be effective in the vacuous darkness of the cave. We begin to realize that in the austere emptiness of the cave, we will have to become empty ourselves, and that is, perhaps, the fiercest terror of all. Amazingly, however, when we face that ultimate terror, we're surprised to find that the small, enclosed, darkened prison of the cave becomes, in the words of e.e. cummings, "the enormous room." This is what the Desert Fathers wanted their disciples to discover, and they knew that the only way this discovery could be made was to resist the temptation to leave the cave too quickly.

We come to the desert to empty out our over-filled and over-manipulated lives, but what we uncover is the limitation of manipulation. The desert is raw and it leaves us raw. We're shaved and shaped like the cave that has been carved and chiseled by the slow action of moving ground water that eventually dissolves even rock, or the molten liquid that has flowed continuously within a hardened lava tube creating beautifully sculptured blackened caves. We're ragged and wounded but left beautifully empty to await the fullness of the Holy One. After we've dumped out our worldly fullness, the desert takes what's left, strips it bare, and prepares us for fullness. We have no real part in the process, other than going to the desert cave and staying there. No manipulation on our part is able to create within us what the cave offers so freely and abundantly.

What happens, of course, is that we finally dip our toes into the glassy water of humility. The water of humility that silently calls us as surely as a still pond allures us in summer's heat. We know intuitively that if we approach that water, we will be able to see to the bottom, but even more importantly we will see a true picture of our own face. That's what humility really is—seeing the true picture of our own face. We're usually so clever at not truly looking at ourselves that we're often astonished when we're confronted with our authentic self. Surprisingly, when we have nothing more to prove, when we have no more need to claim status and prestige, when we can accept that we're not perfect and can't please every-one, when we stop trying to be something or someone other than what we've been created to be, we become as clear and pure and whole as a child freshly born. All that we've done to keep our true self hidden seems strangely unnecessary, as we begin to see our-selves through God's eyes. We no longer need to try to cover up what we fear is so inadequate, because when we see ourselves through God's eyes, we see that what God created is good.

This is the humility that characterized the life of Jesus. He was able to refrain from falling into the seductive temptations placed before him when he was being prepared for his ministry because he saw himself through the eyes of heaven. He was able to refrain from public accolades and adulation because he saw himself through the eyes of heaven. He was able to refrain from defending himself at his mock trial because he saw himself through the eyes of heaven. He was able to refrain from hating his enemies and those who executed him because he saw himself through the eyes of heaven. When we've experienced the emptiness that is found in the desert cave, we move toward that true humility, ready to accept the invitation to yield to what is greater than ourselves. We're willing to see the higher purpose of our life. We're unafraid to risk for the sake of love. We're open to new possibilities for finding meaning in life. We are confident that life is not ended in death. This didn't happen for me after spending one uneasy night in a desert cave. What I learned from that one night, however, is that the uneasiness would only dissipate when I was content to remain in the unfamiliar place longer than I thought I could—only then would it become familiar enough that I could draw out the lessons it had to teach. If we can ride through the uneasiness, we can find our entire soul slowly and subtly sliding into a place of readiness for what is peering at us just over the pinkish horizon of the desert morning.

A Prayer Practice for Moving from Emptying to Emptiness: Part I

When first we go to the desert to empty ourselves of the excesses of our lives, we spill out the contents of our heart as if we were expelling water after having nearly drowned. Once all the toxins have been vomited out, we take a deep breath and allow our body and soul to relax. There is, within us, a feeling of having accomplished what we came to do. Just as we are too quick to leave a desert cave, so we can too quickly depart from the desert scape after we've emptied everything out there. But when we stay, we begin to understand that being empty is not emptiness. The agenda of becoming empty of stress, anxiety, overwork, unrealistic demands and expectations gives way to God's agenda to foster in us an emptiness that leads to true humility. This practice is meant to take us to that deeper level of emptiness where humility seeps into us, and we're finally free from being anything or anyone other than what we are.

To begin the practice, set aside an hour and go to a place of quiet. Choose an empty church sanctuary, a secluded space in your home, or a park bench in the sun. After you have settled yourself, become aware of the scents and sounds around you. Note any stress that you are holding in your body. Bring your attention to the deep well within your soul and observe whether or not you feel any distortion or disturbance there. Take a few deep breaths and ask the Holy One to assure you of being in the Divine Presence. Enter the place of memories in your mind and recall a time when you felt a great emptiness in your life, but an emptiness that left you feeling content. Visualize the features of that emptiness: what brought you to it, how you felt as you went from fullness to emptiness, who participated in the experience, how long your contentment lasted. Try to relive even the smallest details of the memory. Do not be alarmed if salty tears drop down your cheeks, or if your heart's beat feels uneven, or if you feel a tingling sensation near the surface of your skin. Often the most profound suffering is the gateway to the emptiness that leaves the soul at peace. Remembering the elements of such suffering can leave you feeling weak and weepy. Being in a quiet place alone will give you the freedom to feel your emotions fully.

A Prayer Practice for Moving from Emptying to Emptiness: Part II

Maybe you don't have a cave in a mountain nearby where you can go for an extended period of time, but you can recreate the cave as a cell in your home. You might use your desert place for this part of the practice, or an isolated corner of a quiet room, or an empty closet. The space doesn't necessarily need to be small, but it does need to be separate from other trafficked areas. It needs to be bare but beautiful. The desert cave's décor is minimalist, but its bare ruggedness exudes a stark beauty all its own. Take time to prepare your cell so that it feels as beautifully empty as your soul will become by spending time in it. After you've lovingly and prayerfully created your "cave," spend thirty minutes each day for the next five days in it doing the following exercise.

- Become aware of your surroundings, noting the feel of the space, the silence and separation, the light or lack of it, the absence of stimulation. Pay attention to any anxiety, uneasiness, or boredom that may be tickling your mind and soul. Try to still your soul and imagine that you are being held inside a safe cavity that has been cut into solid rock.
- The air inside the cavity is none other but the Spirit of God and every time you breathe in, you are breathing in that Spirit. And,

every time you breathe out, your breath is becoming one with that Spirit. Take at least ten minutes to focus on your breath: breathe in the Spirit, breathe out into the Spirit, breathe in the Spirit, breathe out into the Spirit, breathe in the Spirit, breathe out into the Spirit.

- Sing or whisper the words to the third verse of the familiar hymn "Rock of Ages":

While I draw this fleeting breath, when mine eyelids close in death,
When I rise to worlds unknown and behold thee on thy throne,
Rock of ages, cleft for me, let me hide myself in thee.[6]

- Read the following Scripture from the book of Job very slowly.
  Day 1: Job 38
  Day 2: Job 39
  Day 3: Job 40
  Day 4: Job 41
  Day 5: Job 42

- Reflect on the following questions each day and write a few notes of response in your journal.

What are the first feelings that arise in me as I read the Scripture passage?
What does this passage tell me about God?
What does it tell me about myself?
How does this passage wound me and heal me at the same time?
Where do I need to yield in my life in order to see the true picture of my own face?

- Take ten minutes to attend to the feelings of true humility. Here you are in a room where you are unseen and unknown. A place where you experience the limitation of your own manipulation. There is no possibility of covering your soul with the clothes you

6. The Hymnal 1982 (New York: The Church Hymnal Corporation, 1985), 685.

are so accustomed to wearing in front of others. Your soul is as naked before God as it was when you were first formed in the womb. Feel the wonder of that nascent soul. See it through the eyes of God. Don't leave the cave (even if the thirty minutes are up!) if you haven't come to a point of humble stillness in your soul. When you're that still, you'll feel nothing but the love of the Holy One swirling around you like fog over the coast on a summer afternoon.

CHAPTER 10

From Embrace to Release

Most of us, when thinking about living a simpler life, have thought about what we'd take with us for six months on an isolated island. The top item on my list would be my Christmas tin box that I inherited from my grandmother. It sits in my kitchen; actually, it's been in every one of my kitchens for the last forty years. It doesn't matter where I am in the whole world; when I close my eyes and lift the lid of that tin, the unmistakably pungent but delightful scent of the desert wafts out, and I am immediately in the place where my soul is at home. I think I would easier part with a limb than that tin. What has been in that tin these many years are the dried leaves of the creosote bush, also known as the chaparral or greasewood bush. My grandmother was enamored with alternative health practices, and drinking the tea of the chaparral was one of them. The ancient Native people made wide use of the tea as a tonic and cure for various ailments. The plant contains a very strong antioxidant thought to prevent cancer. My grandmother was certain that drinking the tea would keep her healthy. Since the creosote bush is so prolific in the Southwest desert regions, she had an endless supply right outside her back door. Every morning she took a vigorous five-mile walk in the desert, and on many of the hottest mornings, she would cut the stems from a creosote bush, tie them in small bunches, and hang them to dry in the scalding sun. To retain the strength of their healing properties, she kept the dried leaves in dark tins, until she needed to steep them for her tea. As a child, I loved to open those tins to smell the leaves. There's controversy these days about the advisability of drinking chaparral tea for physical health, but there is no doubt that the Christmas tin box of dried leaves has kept my soul in health for many, many years. And surprisingly, miraculously, the scent is as strong now as it was when I used to sneak a smell as a child.

While the intoxicating fragrance of the ubiquitous creosote bush is memorable, the lessons that the creosote can teach us go far beyond mere scent. The loveliness of the odor that spreads through the air after the falling of rain is a path of cleansing and purification for the bush. If truth be told, the creosote has adapted and survived because it has learned how to keep others away. The very word *creosote* in Greek means "flesh preserver." The plant is intent on self-survival. It conserves energy by producing resins that coat the leaves and keep water from being sucked away by the hot dry air. It will then drop its leaves in order to safeguard the much-needed moisture within the heart of the plant. While other less resilient desert plants have long since become one with the grains of hot sand, the creosote bush can live for a century or more. When the center stalks wither and die, the outside edges grow new shoots and the plant continues not only to survive but also thrive. It grows like a weed, keeps as much water as possible for itself, and the very resin that prevents the sun from stealing moisture also acts as a protective and toxic defense against mammals and insects that would try to munch away its leaves and branches. The creosote appears to be a very unfriendly part of the flora of the desert because in its desire for self-protection it repels others and keeps the scarce resources for itself. But, on further reflection, this is nothing but an embrace from heaven given to a seemingly selfish little bush. The embrace is real, but like all embraces, temporary. The embrace will eventually lead to release.

The word *release* comes from the Latin word that means "to

loosen, to grow slack, to relax." For all the defenses and toxic
substances that the creosote bush produces to keep other plants
from growing too closely to it, it would be unnatural for it to remain
always in that protective embrace. When the rains come, the bush
is unloosed from the embrace. Its leaves begin to relax—loosen—
under the rain's dampness, and the pungent fragrance is released
into the air as if it were an evening offering of the richest incense.
When the water cleanses the soil beneath the bush, other plants can
grow under it. The embrace of nature offers safety, but before the
bush becomes too comfortable and indulgent in that embrace, the
drops of water that fall from heaven force the leaves to relax. When
they do, they can move into a less self-protective posture and
others can move closer in.

The stress, tension, and overabundance of our lives can leave us
feeling as if we need to push others away in order to maintain our
balance. We can feel a need to garner every sustaining resource for
ourselves just to survive. When we feel our very lifeblood is being
sapped away while we stand by helpless to halt the erosion of
creativity, energy, enthusiasm, and spiritedness, we can become
isolated and unfriendly—a sort of human version of the creosote
bush. We long to spill ourselves out into the arms of the vast landscape and be enfolded in a blanket of safety and security. The desert
does not disappoint. The holy embrace of security and protection
awaits us, but it is temporary. In the fullness of time, the gentle rains
of life will come and when they do we will know that we are being
released from the embrace. Our souls will start to relax, as we are
readied to offer the rare perfume of our lives to the world.

When we're in the throes of what life has so randomly, and
sometimes harshly, dealt out, and find ourselves able to "let go"
into the embrace of God, we find it hard to imagine being released
from that embrace of protection. What we really want is to avoid
returning to the thing we've been trying to escape. Once those
arms of heaven have opened to welcome us in, we can't conceive
of being released back to the continuous struggle of life. "Surely,"
we tell ourselves, "God won't want to release us. If God is the

Lover and Sustainer of our lives, it would be going against God's very nature to release us from the arms that will keep us out of harm's way." Yet unbeknownst to us, the embrace itself prepares us for the release.

After I'd returned to the desert, certain that I'd never leave again, I took the greatest hope and spiritual comfort in burrowing into every familiar and tender embrace that the desert always offers me. I drank in the scent of creosote, I wallowed in the great silence, I sated my hunger for isolation, I took long desert walks in the pre-dawn and before nighttime slumber. I let my mind and soul claim the resources I needed for nourishment, and I kept at arms length everyone who expected more of me than I wanted to give. I listened for the voice of the Spirit of God, and let the burning heat of the desert sear my heart again in love. Then, the call came that I was needed for work in a place far away from the desert. I tried to avoid answering the call, feeling sure the Holy One wouldn't want me to leave the delectable embrace that was giving me such joy. Unfortunately, avoidance works only as long as we remain inattentive to reality. When I finally realized that I was simply avoiding leaving my secure and happy space, it suddenly became clear to me that the holy arms were opening and I was being released. At the moment this was revealed to me, I relaxed. I simply relaxed. Answering the call to take up the new work didn't feel onerous or intrusive any longer. God had readied me for the release from the safe embrace. Joy and anticipation surged through me like an electrical current through copper wire, and I was prepared for what would come next. I made sure, however, that I packed my Christmas tin box of dried creosote leaves!

There's nothing in our lives beyond the seeing eye of the Holy One. There's no inner conflict, fear, stress, loss, or despair beyond the heart of the Holy One. There's no moment when the arms are unwilling to take us in. There is, however, always a moment when the arms open up again to release us. Like the rains that cleanse and purify the creosote bush so that it emits an unforgettable fragrance and does not die from its own self-indulgence and isolation, so the moisture of heaven will drop quietly into our souls to alert us that it is time again to wake from our own tender sleep in the arms of safety, to greet a new day, a new way of being, a new life.

A Prayer Practice for Moving from Embrace to Release: Part I

A friend of mine, after undergoing a stressful situation, went on a trip to Alaska, and on her return commented to me, "I think I found in Alaska what you find in the desert." The embrace of God is never held within limited borders. For one, the desert, for another the ocean, for another the plains, for another the mountains, for another fields of flowers. What is common isn't the topography, but the human need for tangible reminders that will scratch away the film that clouds our distinct and diverse memories of places that have touched us deeply. We all respond to different reminders because our memories are so individual and unique. This prayer practice is designed to help uncover the memories of place that have not only been formed in us through the course of our lived history, but have touched us so deeply that we resonate with them even when we don't know why.

The first part of this practice is to go on a kind of field trip. Take yourself to a local bookstore, or to the library, and saunter over to the area where magazines are displayed. Let your eyes fall on the section of magazines that are nature oriented or indigenous to particular geographical areas. Notice which ones stir up an immediate attraction within you. Pick up two or three and leaf through them. What are the scenes, the colors, the flowers, the landscapes that you are drawn to? Try not to think about what you're looking at. Instead, be very attentive to the feelings that bubble up in you as you look at the various terrains and environments. Purchase or borrow one or two of the magazines to take home with you.

A Prayer Practice for Moving from Embrace to Release: Part II

- Set aside at least thirty minutes and take your journal and new magazine with you to your desert place.
- Quiet yourself and feel the presence of the Holy One moving gently in you and around you by taking some smooth, slow breaths. Ask the Holy One to open your senses and help you uncover the memories of place that lie hidden within your soul.
- Read the following verses from Scripture: Jeremiah 2:6; Hosea 14:5; Psalm 107:23, 24; and Exodus 34:2, 3. Note in your journal which single one immediately seems to nudge your soul with delight, curiosity, or desire. Jot down any other feelings or thoughts that rise up in you.
- Spend a few minutes with your magazine(s), looking at the pictures with attention and intention. Again, note which ones seem to immediately nudge your soul with delight, curiosity, or desire and write down your reflections in your journal.
- Close your eyes and imagine that you and the Holy One are going to meet somewhere in nature. Observe the images that flow into the corners of your mind. You may find you're immediately aware of a scene from your childhood, or a scene of a favorite vacation spot, or a scene of a place you like to go to escape the rigors of the world, or a place you find difficult to leave. Once the place is set in your mind, allow yourself to sit quietly in it. Try to imagine as many details as you can. What is the temperature? Is the sun shining, or is the sky overcast? Are there particular scents that emerge? What colors do you see in the environment? Is the air clear or is fog swirling around? Do you feel closed in and safe, or is your safety found in the openness? After a few minutes allow your imagination to fall on a particular feature that you see in the space. It might be a rock, or a flower, or a branch, or a shell, or a blade of grass, or a stalk of wheat. Imagine picking up the item and turn it over in your hand, noting its various aspects. Reverently, place it back in its appointed place.

- Now, close your eyes and imagine that the Holy One has entered the place and you are no longer alone. As the Holy One comes and sits near you, again pick up the item that you were just holding. Ask the Holy One why you feel drawn to this place and to this item, and what you might learn from it. After you feel a stream of clarity and stillness filling your soul, thank the Holy One for the time you have spent together.
- After you've opened your eyes, look through the magazine again to see if there's a picture of an item similar to the one you picked up. If you find one, cut it out and put it in your desert place until you are able to procure an actual one. If you don't find one in the magazine, try sketching one in your journal, cut it out, and put it in the desert place. Let the image become a touchstone for you—a touchstone that will take you to the embrace of God and sustain you when you've been released from that embrace.

CHAPTER 11

From Identity to Belonging

It was a way of honoring what is at the heart of belonging—presence. It was a way of connecting with the habitat they'd created, a part of my own history somewhere in the collective unconscious. I donned my soft deerskin moccasins the color of sand, beaded by the painstaking work of a member of the Shoshone tribe of Eastern Idaho. It wasn't the wearing of the moccasins alone that formed the connection or offered the dignity. It was walking in those moccasins in the desert climes and ruins that had held the print of hand-stitched moccasins centuries before. So, when the day had broken into full bloom, I would carefully tie my moccasins and go to the Sinagua Indian ruins known as "Tuzigoot" that was perched in the high desert on top of a ridge near my own desert dwelling. The first time my feet traipsed up the walkway to the ruins, it was early morning, and tourists hadn't yet stepped forth from their hotel rooms. I was blissfully alone—alone with the great sky, the bordered horizon, the uneven rocks, the grand vista, the humble desert shrubs, and the silence that stretched not only across the land but across the centuries. After climbing to the top and coming around the backside of the pueblo remnants that were built by the Sinagua between1100 and 1400 CE, I felt as if I already knew the place. I sat down on a visitor's bench and I felt them—the Sinagua.

I heard the voice of their spirits. I watched their children playing.
I saw their sun-worn skin that had the texture and color of worn
leather. I glimpsed their smiles as they danced and played under the
moon's opalescent light. I winced at the weary sadness in their faces
as they made the decision to abandon the place. They just left one
day—no one knows why. The very word *tuzigoot*—an Apache word
for "crooked water"—may offer a clue. They departed and the only
residue of their sojourn on that mountain ridge are the ruins and the
palpable beat of their spirits. I wrote the poem "Desert Dwellers" as
my own acknowledgment of their lives and their presence:

While popes and kings in Europe
Debate issues of Church and state,
You sit on your desert mesa
Watching light's day fall from the sky
And moon's rise clothe the night.

Scouts scan the sandy landscape
Your women weave your desert wear.
Children play games that children know,
And sun beats relentlessly
Drying your desert floor.

Arid soil becomes your clay,
Rocks and sand form your pueblos.
Saltbrush and winterfat make dyes
To paint your petroglyph tale,
Left for a future day.

Lives are conceived and given birth,
Earth's joy lifted to Spirit God.
The plaza your nighttime playground,
Dusty hills your hunting ground.

Then one day you are gone.

Oh, Sinagua ancestors,
Was desert death your destruction?
Was Tuzigoot her treach'rous self?
Were your lips parched in hard sun?
Your deep thirst left unquenched?

Or, in the silence of night
Did another desert call you?
Did ears empty hear Spirit's voice?
And rise like old Abraham
To follow Spirit's choice?[7]

Nearly every day I would go to Tuzigoot to meditate, and always before meditating, I took note of their presence—their "belonging" in the place. Through them I learned that presence is intimately connected to belonging. Belonging is certainly about connecting with the landscape, but at an even deeper level it is about recognizing the oneness shared with a reality beyond the landscape. It's an awareness of—and relationship with—the greater reality of presence that's both held within the landscape and eternally distinct from it.

The desert bears this truth more intensely than other topographies, perhaps because of the harshness of its environment where presence seems always to be vulnerable and at risk. Desert life over the long haul is a teeter-totter business. It can't be counted on. It's depleting and demanding. While the desert can't be taken for granted, it's also true that when the tender footsteps of desert dwellers have once touched the variable grains of sand, the sands do not forget that they've been touched. The dry and fickle land may require dwellers to disperse, but it holds on to souls and sprinkles their soul dust amid the grains of sand so that nothing is lost or even forgotten. That's why I knew the Sinagua were there with me that first day. They may have had to give up the desert, but the desert did not give them up. Their presence would be held like a

---

7. Renee Miller, "Desert Dwellers," in *A Brief Moment of Infinite Time* (self published), 30.

precious ointment that could offer a soothing balm to other travelers through earth who had mistaken or lost their belonging.

Even now, whenever I'm away from the desert, I keep a picture of Tuzigoot nearby, so that I remember their presence—the belonging of the Sinagua. And, when I feel I have lost my compass point of direction and am wandering aimlessly like an android through the pathways of life, I stop and settle into their presence and recall again that my belonging is centered in the place that holds my deepest longing and my deepest presence.

Daily life can leave us feeling severed from the reality of presence and belonging. The more technological we become the more we are cut off from our belonging with the earth that forms us. You only have to look at pictures of ancient people to see that the lines in their faces and the pigments of their skin seem to mirror the lines and colors of the earth. But, we have become so disconnected that it is sometimes difficult even to identify the earth as our mother. The very wildness of the desert, its teeming energy hidden under the disguise of sameness, its insistent and stern intensity will never allow us to forget our roots in the earth. Other tamer topographies offer instead a respite and recreation from the angst that skids around the edges of our lives. In more domesticated landscapes there are trees to climb, and limbs to swing from. There are cool lakes and streams where our heated bodies can swim and frolic. There are fields of flowers where we can forget our beige computers and lose ourselves in the rowdiness of color. There are oceans where we can scout through wet sand for shells and treasure. There are grasses where we can lie and stare at the shapes of clouds.

The desert offers none of these amusements. If we go there looking for the attractions of other topographies, we'll be disappointed, even disillusioned. Even the breathing space from life that the desert does offer is a harsh one. When we go to the desert to regain our sense of balance and clear ourselves of the unnecessary dross that's accumulated in our lives, we won't find the desert a place of comfort. The desert will give us nothing less than an experience of the reality that we came from earth and to earth we will return.

There will be no soft mounds of grass or cool rivers to wade in, but the desert will open us to the meaning of belonging, which is grounded in longing and presence. Part of the reason we flee to the desert is that we know intuitively that for the days we're treading the byways of earth we will be longing for what's real and true, for what will fill the echoing emptiness inside us, for what will open the doors of meaning to what seems senseless, for what will tell us our place and our purpose, for what will answer the existential yearning that ceaselessly cries silently within our soul. We can choose to sweat through our frustration as if we were scraping paint from an old weathered house, or we can simply accept the fact that for the years we inhabit this world we will be longing. That longing is actually the key to our belonging. Look at it this way: consider the place that you call "home"—the place that feels comfortable and safe to you, the place where your heart feels settled and secure. When you're away from that home—particularly in a place of unresolved issues and unanswered questions—you long for home, you yearn for home, your soul cries for home. The very longing itself makes it clear where you belong. A disciple once asked a wise desert woman, "Amma, I came to the desert to answer the questions of my soul, but no answers come." The desert mother told the disciple to walk the desert floor until his heart became still. The disciple walked through the desolate landscape day after day, but found no peace. He went to the Amma and asked what to do. She told him to go and walk the city streets until his heart became still. There he walked day after day amidst the colors and noise of the crowded city. At first, he was excited by the city and found that his questions no longer troubled him. But as he continued walking, the same old questions rose in him again, and then one day he knew he wanted to go back to the desert. He returned to the Amma. "Did your heart become still? Were the questions of your soul answered?" she asked. "No," said the man. "But, the more I walked the more I longed to be in the place where I belong." "Ah," said the Amma. "Then you have found the answer to your questions. In your longing is your belonging."

Jesus said that where our treasure is, there our heart will be also. If we rinse our heart out until there is nothing but treasure, we'll find that the essence of that treasure is held in the bond of presence between who and what has gone before us, and in the bond between our longing and our belonging. The desert will never allow us to forget reality, but neither will it forget or forsake us. Our longing will drive us to it. In it we will experience presence. Through it we will find our true belonging.

A Prayer Practice for Moving from Identity to Belonging: Part I

Our lives in contemporary society move at breakneck speed. We're barely aware of the presence of those in our own family, much less those who no longer physically inhabit this earth. Yet, understanding where and how we belong in this world is centered first on the connection of presence that we experience not only with the earth, but with the ancestors who have gone before us. Our limited understanding keeps us from even entertaining the idea that we can experience the presence of those who have already died. We're like Martha who, when asked by Jesus if she believed in the resurrection, said that she knew her dead brother would rise again at the last day. We may believe intellectually that we'll be reunited with the dead for eternity, but we have little trust of experiencing now the presence of those who have died. This part of the practice will help open you to the presence of those who are all around you, even though they are hid from your physical sight.

- First, identify a historical landmark near you. It might be a building, a museum, a roadside where something momentous occurred, a graveyard of an important personage, a national monument. Choose a time to go to the site when the fewest visitors or tourists will be there, so that you can enter more deeply into the experience.
- Before you go, do some research about the event that occurred there, or the people who were a part of the place. You can uncover

plenty of information at your local library, from the agency in charge of the site, and from the Internet.

- As you arrive, be attentive to opening yourself to what is beyond yourself. You might even imagine that you have been put into a time machine and are now in a prior time and history.

- Find a place where you can sit quietly. Focus on your breath for a few moments and ask God to enlarge your boundaries so that you can recognize the timelessness of eternity in the here and now.

- Take a look at your surroundings, noting the scents, textures, and any changes that may have occurred over the years in that place.

- Close your eyes and imagine a scene from a prior day in that place. Picture the people, the energy, the daily activity, the sounds of the place. Listen carefully for the presence of those you've come to see. Pretend you're a newcomer. Ask questions of people who may have once been in the place and write in your journal any insights that you receive.

- After you feel there's no more information to digest, thank the people and the place for being present to you. Thank God who has made it possible for you to feel the boundless presence of eternity.

- Try writing a short poem about the people and place you've visited.

A Prayer Practice for Moving from Identity to Belonging: Part II

Our belonging is to our longing what the current is to the stream. They are so intimately connected that each needs the other for its fulfillment. This part of the practice will help you identify the pockets of longing waiting to be lined with the fullness of belonging— of knowing where your place is in this world. Take your journal with you to your desert place and plan to spend at least thirty minutes there.

- As you enter your desert place take a few moments to sit quietly and notice what the place does *not* offer and make a note of this in your journal.

- Close your eyes and be attentive to the feeling of every muscle in your body. Tighten and relax your muscles one by one, paying attention to the space between the tightening and the relaxing. This is the space of longing—the space where you are ready to let go of the tight feeling, but have not yet grasped the feeling of limpness in the muscle.

- Ask God to pull away the curtain that you use to keep your longing from overwhelming you. Tell God what your fears are about your longing, and why you want to keep it hidden from others and yourself.

- Spend a few minutes reading and reflecting on Psalm 63:1–4:

*O God, you are my God; eagerly I seek you; ***
  my soul thirsts for you, my flesh faints for you,
  as in a barren and dry land where there is no water.
*Therefore I have gazed upon you in your holy place, ***
  that I might behold your power and your glory.
*For your loving-kindness is better than life itself; ***
  my lips shall give you praise.
*So I will bless you as long as I live ***
  and lift up my hands in your Name.

- Write your thoughts about the following questions in your journal:

When do I feel an empty ache in my soul?
What do I do to satisfy the ache?
When do I feel fullness in my soul?
Who and for what am I existentially homesick?

- End your time in your desert place by drawing a picture, or writing a poem, or simply making a few notes in your journal about when you feel your longing and your belonging meet.

CHAPTER 12

From Darkness to Light

It's the in-between times that are charged with the particles of untold grace. We're often surprisingly unaware of those moments, not because they're not important, but because they get lost in the shuffle of getting from what *was* to what *will be*. One of the most important gifts the desert offers is its insistence on paying attention to those in-between times. The very lack of stimulation in the stretch of sand—the absence of color, the lack of contrasts, the mere outward show of quiet demeanor—creates one of two responses in us. Either we pass it by as if it were just another blurry gray day and let our energy and enthusiasm be drawn to what *does* offer some kind of vigorous stimulation. Or, we single-mindedly scout the landscape for some kind of alteration, some movement, some sign that life is pulsing in the apparently drear and dead land. The desert rarely allows us to choose the first response. In other landscapes it takes discipline to attend to the delicate and faint changes that are regularly occurring. We get so involved in our daily activities that we're barely aware of what's going on around us in our environment. How many of us, for example, have never even visited the geographical landmarks closest to our front door? But what is merely a faint change in another topography is bold and strong in the desert, and it's much more difficult to turn a blind eye and a deaf ear to the movement that unfolds. So, rather than simply passing the desert by, we find ourselves stalking it like a sly cat—staying on the lookout for what is different, what is moving, what is evolving, what has the potential of keeping us "awake." Because we're intentional about finding that movement, we can be much more aware of the in-between moments. The *work* of desert life, however, becomes discovering the gold nuggets buried in those moments.

One of the first in-between times is the half-come time of day—the time when the night is giving way to the dawn—when the darkness hasn't given its final bow and the light hasn't yet made its showstopping entrance onto the stage. The movement in the half-come time of day is so slow and subtle that we can find ourselves bored before it reaches its grand conclusion. At first awed by the beauty, the mystery, the other-worldliness of it, our attention spans are short and we find it difficult to remain focused. We find our body anxious to move, our voice ready to be released into the air, our stomach hungry for nourishment, our mind ready for tackling the tasks of the day. We just want the light to come. We just want to get going—get on with the business at hand. We want results, not progress. We want an outcome, not a process. We're uneasy when nothing has really yet ended and nothing has really yet begun. This is the insidious danger—not only at pre-dawn in the desert, but in all the in-between times of our lives—especially when we're waiting for the light to snuff out the darkness of our lives.

When I was just beginning my adult life—hovering still between adolescence and the world of maturity—the desert made me pay attention to the eddy of activity going on during that in-between time of my life. It was the pre-dawn, the half-come time of day, more than any other aspect of the desert, that awakened me to the understated but crucial action occurring within me. Like many teenagers struggling with hormonal and emotional changes, I'd find myself sleeping hours and hours at a time, and then I'd find myself wide awake when everyone else was snuggled tightly in blissful slumber. When such spurts of insomnia washed over me, I'd get up just when the darkness had decided it was time for its act to end. I'd walk to the large window that opened out toward the desert mountain range in the eastern sky. I'd be mesmerized during the time it took for the light to finally come. The black darkness shifted to a dull gunmetal gray, and at the same time, the softest shades of pink and orange organza fabric were slowly but surely raised. The coming of light at day's dawn is in the same palette as the coming of evening and the emergence of darkness, but there's no mistaking the difference between the two. The colors at sun's set are audacious, like the last flourish of the artist's paint on the unfinished canvas, while those at dawn are like a wispy feather softly stroking the sky. When I watched the stroking of the sky, with a patience that even now astounds me, I felt the stroking of my own soul. I think I learned I really had a soul during that half-come time of day. It was there that my adolescent emotions that were as nubby and rough as burlap were gently smoothed into something as refined as elegant velvet. It was then that I began to understand that my life would take on enormous changes as I stepped into adulthood and it was then that I caught a whiff of the meaning of my life in its broader context. I wrote at that time:

> *what more beauty could there be, than this,*
> *That God is letting me see . . .*
> *It's so beauteous I want to cry,*
> *But I need something to live by . . .*
> *Soon the sunrise is through*
> *And then, the day closes too.*
> *What do you think I now see?*
> *The sunset, which is a reflection of me.*

I can't say that I am now unswervingly aware of the in-between times of my life, but I know that those times hold within them the deeper mystery of the meaning of our lives, the purpose of our lives, the possibilities and potentialities of our lives. It's at those times that we're most open to the action of the Holy One in our lives. It's then that we're like a book waiting to be written by the hand of God.

When we feel overcome with the presence of darkness in our lives, it's as if the light is continually beyond us, always out of our reach. When we cease to crave and demand the light, and are content to learn the lessons taught in the space between the dark and the light, we begin to touch the deepest part of our soul. At times we may feel like the darkness in our lives has left us as strings unstruck, unsung, unimagined, but in those in-between times the light of the Holy One slides across us like the bow on a Stradivarius creating a melody that we could have only dimly imagined.

The desert was often featured in the stories of Scripture when people were walking in darkness and waiting for the light to dawn in their lives. The Israelites experienced such an in-between time when they wandered for forty years in the desert between the ending of their slavery in Egypt and their new entry into the Promised Land. Jonah experienced it when he was stuck in the "desert" of the whale's belly for three days and nights—between the call of God and his willingness to live that call. The disciples experienced it in the "desert" time between the death of Jesus and his resurrection. We too easily focus on the results in these accounts—the light dawning after a time of darkness—but it was in the space between the darkness and the coming of light that the hand and heart of God were massaging and shaping lives with threads of grace.

When the sun's rays have burned away the last trace of darkness in the eastern desert sky, and the day has fully come, it feels as if the darkness in our lives has slid away just as silently and easily. Dropping our souls down into the desert sand, in the half-come time of day, helps us recognize that the dark and the light are a balanced movement. Each has something to give, something to teach, some grace to bestow. When we can entrust ourselves to this process, we'll no longer need to do everything we can to avoid darkness, nor will we need to curse the presence of darkness in our lives, nor will we seek to cover up its presence under the guise of false and ineffective emotional masks. We can trust that the darkness is what it is, and the light is what it is. We can wait through the in-between time knowing that it is the time of unseen growth. We need only sit and wait. In its time, the day will dawn as surely as the spring rains cover the earth.

A Prayer Practice for Moving from Darkness to Light

In many ways the in-between times in our lives are "deserts" of their own, even if they don't take place in a geographical desert. They're often times when we feel isolated and confused, times when we're scouring our lives for the slightest change that will assure us that there's movement in the bland and uninteresting terrain of our soul, times when the Holy One feels strangely and fearfully absent, times when we want to do anything else but be still and wait for the light to dawn. This part of the practice will give you a pattern for re-entering in-between times that you have already experienced in your life. Exploring what was gained there—even if you were unaware of it at the time—will give you a way to recognize and even look forward to the in-between times that still wait on the horizon of your life.

Schedule an hour to spend in your desert place. Take only your journal and pen and your soul, ready to go back in time. When you first sit down, spend a few moments thinking about an in-between time for you. It might have been deciding on whether or not to take a new job, or living through the loss of someone you loved, or hearing news of a dread illness, or during a time of pregnancy, or the betrayal of someone you trusted, or the decision whether or not to marry. Most likely, several such in-between times will come to mind. Choose one for this prayer practice and note it in your journal, then proceed through the process below.

- Close your eyes and imagine sitting in a dry and monotonous desert. The sand is dotted with untended bushes only a shade different than the sand's color and that's all you can see for miles, except for a small desert hill a few hundred yards away. While the landscape seems devoid of action, you can sense a presence that pulses even through the dull view—the presence of God. Take a few moments to center on that pulsing presence. Give your heart and attention to it. Feel it surrounding and enfolding you, even as your own breath and heartbeat slow. Ask God to help you see the grace that has been at work in the seemingly inactive times of your life.

- Shift your focus by imagining that you're climbing the small desert hill. When you reach the top and look over, you find yourself in another place, another time. You see the geography of where you experienced the in-between time you chose earlier for this exercise. You sit down and see in that geography someone who looks surprisingly like you did when you were living through that time. Watch yourself from afar, paying attention to the sounds, people, and emotions that fill that person you're watching.

- Write down the details that you see, asking yourself such questions as: What's going on in this scene? What's the darkness? What are the questions? What's the urgency that's felt? Where's the avoidance? What's the frustration?

- Fast forward to when the situation was resolved and the light was revealed. Write down the details that you see, asking yourself such questions as: What's going on in this scene? What caused the light? What did it feel like once the questions were answered? How did excitement and energy fill you? How did gratitude overtake you?

- Now, watch carefully to see yourself during the time between the darkness and the light. Write down the details that you see, asking yourself such questions as: Where was God present? How was your soul being prepared for the coming of light? What did you need to learn? Who stayed with you and encouraged you through the process? What would you have missed had you not been given the in-between time? How could you have been more aware, more attentive, more open to the slow, but steady movement of that in-between time?

• After you've written until you know there's nothing more to record, turn around and go back down the other side of the hill and into the featureless desert. Sit very still again in the presence of the Holy One. Offer a prayer of thanksgiving for the lessons that are shared and the grace that is given during the times in your life when darkness slowly sheds its skin and, when the time is right, the light rises because your soul is ready to be clothed with sun.

CHAPTER 13

From Sound to Sharing

The time always comes. We go to the desert in search of something, and the desert seems to be expecting us. It seems to be always there waiting to share its silence and its sound. Its arms are ever outstretched in an eternal welcome to any and all who need to be enfolded into the silence beyond time, and to those who then need to scratch the surface deeper, to hear the sounds of life hid from all but the most attentive and aware. The desert offers no judgment. It doesn't insist that we hurry to get as much silence as possible in the shortest amount of time. It doesn't require us to experience all the unique sounds it has to offer, or depart from its borders so it can return to its own business undisturbed. The desert extends what it has to give without apology, without explanation, without expectation, without preconceived agendas, without sacrificing to the place where it has nothing more to give. It gives only and always what it can, with no begrudging of the gift. It doesn't try to be anything but what it is and it doesn't try to give anything it doesn't really and authentically possess. The desert, though harsh, is really the ideal hostess to all who have the courage to go beyond what is known, familiar, comfortable, and comforting.

The time always comes. When we step away from civilization and drop ourselves into the drear and dread land, we notice first the great deep silence. While we're there, we begin to hear the sounds that belong uniquely to the desert, but there comes the moment when the desert returns to the immense silence, and we know it's time to leave. The desert has given all it will give at present and its silence is the signal. The sounds of the desert that we've strained so hard to hear, and have finally identified and appropriated to ourselves, meld into the landscape so softly and enigmatically that there's no longer any distinction between the sounds we tried so hard to hear in the immense silence and the silence itself. The silence has become sound and has returned to silence again, and new sounds await us outside the desert. We'll hear those new sounds but we'll hear and participate in them differently than before because our ego has been altered by the desert experience. What we'll share with the world as a result of our time in cosmic desert silence will be different in form and in substance than it would've been had we never crept into that rugged embrace of desolation.

The ideal host has done more than merely provide us a place and space to examine our lives—our impulses, our motivations, our distorted thought patterns and habits of behavior. We've been given something we couldn't have uncovered outside the desert's hot sandy edges. The desert helped re-shape and re-form us so that we'd be able to adapt to the environment to which we'd return. It's made us into a kind of human xerophyte. Many desert plants, including cacti, are known as xerophytes. Xerophytes alter their physical structure in order to adapt to their desert environs. The certain shortness of water supply requires plants to store and conserve every drop of water they can in order to survive. Xerophytes have altered their structure to accommodate themselves to their stark and stressful environment. They have developed shallow root systems, for example, so that they can take water in very quickly and then store it in the center of their stems, their roots, and their spines. They can actually continue living for years on the water that they soak up during one rainfall. Unlike other plants, they've adapted by having few, if any, leaves that could release precious water back into the air. Their prickly spines not only act like needles that suck in and hold the water, but also protect them from animals and provide shade from the blistering sun. Finally, they develop a waxy skin that can retain the scarce and needed moisture. These adaptations make it possible for them to endure a wasteland existence.

This is one great gift of the desert to us. We find in its acrimonious nature a hospitality that gives us what we'll need when we leave. Our desert sojourn helps us develop shallow roots so that we can quickly receive the nourishment we need, storing it in the pockets of our heart and soul to be drawn on when we're no longer traipsing through beige-colored sand. Like the cacti, we can live for years on just one desert feeding. Or, like the prophet Elijah, we can metaphorically go in the strength of that food for "forty days and forty nights." The desert experience also helps us develop spines that will nourish and protect us in the vulnerable and unsafe days and nights that will surely come after we have left the desert. And like those clever xerophytes, we find that desert sun has given the skin of our soul a new texture. We're no longer so defenseless against the whims and vagaries of those in our environment who threaten to rob our soul of the strength and nourishment needed to keep us alive in God.

But the time always comes. It's not that the desert casts us out, but it becomes clear to us that the desert has given all she has to give for now. Even though we're unsure of what we'll encounter back in our everyday lives, we may want to leave. In other words, we're not sad when we go. Our soul knows it's time—a soft memory gathers around us and promises to hold us as we leave— and that silence lets us step away from the arms that have given us so much. We really need not fear the re-entry into our regular lives, because we'll return fuller because of how we've changed along the way.

We'll have learned that the real goal of entering the silence of the desert wasn't so much to get away from the stress and noise of our overactive lives and imaginations, but to clearly see the hardness that had grown over our own souls, hiding our true self. The fissures in the dry clods of desert earth that have seemed so severe have revealed to us that we ourselves have become cracked and fissured. Our souls have begun to look like a loaf of European bread whose crust is so hard that it seems impossible to believe that the inside is soft and pliable, moist and delicate. Once the dry emptiness shows us the beauty of our true selves, we can leave, ready to do as the desert does—offer hospitality to every person or creature that steps across the rims of our lives. Much of the stress and noise of our lives that drove us to the desert silence in the first place drove us precisely because we weren't comfortable being ourselves—offering only and always what we are—without apology, without explanation, without expectation. We'd become used to accommodating ourselves to what others want from us—what the media tells us we should be and do, what our career demands us to be, what we've been taught as children to be, what we ideally think we should be. There is sometimes a chasm between meeting those expectations and the reality of our true selves. The "disconnect" is sometimes so strong that, like an overload in the grid of an electric power plant, we "blow out." Our psychic and spiritual edges are left hot and frayed. We feel we have to flee—to escape the noise that the tumult has brought. In the desert where we are plunged into the dark and endless silence, we're at first discomfited and uneasy, but when we begin to settle into it, the heat of our souls begins to cool, and our frayed edges are soothed. The sounds of the desert begin to re-mold us and we begin to see ourselves anew. Once separated from the false self we've become so accustomed to displaying, we begin to catch a glimpse of our true self and are both surprised and pleased at what we find. We sense a clarity about our humanity and our holiness that we didn't possess before, and when we've reached that new place of understanding, the desert lets us know we can leave our place of quarantine and take our re-found selves back into the world. There, instead of simply falling prey to all the old tapes that informed our previous false self, we have the possibility of maintaining a sense of our true self, and others can begin to find their peace around us. When we return to our regular routines of life, we don't necessarily share through words the lessons we learned in the desert. Rather we share the hospitality of desert silence that helped us recover the authenticity of our true selves.

> A brother came to see a certain hermit and, as he was leaving, he said, "Forgive me, abba, for preventing you from keeping your rule." The hermit replied, "My rule is to welcome you with hospitality and to send you away in peace."[8]

When we have released our expectations and requirements for others and no longer allow those expectations and requirements to drive our interactions, we become the open arms of the desert for others. Then they, too, can catch a glimpse of their true selves and move on in peace.

A Prayer Practice for Moving from Sound to Sharing

Because we're social beings, and most often communicate with one another through words, we're naturally tempted to use that pattern to share our desert experience. When we boldly leave our normal existence in order to slide down into the deep world of desert silence, we know intuitively that we will be changed. When through the silence we begin to be carried on the gentle floating raft of the sound of heaven, we see that we are learning things that had eluded us before. When the sound that's altered us returns to utter noiselessness and we know that it's time to leave the desert, we're eager to express to others what's happened to us, how we've been transformed, how the Holy One has intervened in our lives, and how others can find the same touch of God in their own lives. While this may be a suitable process for other experiences in our lives, it isn't the most helpful response to the gifts we were given by

8. Benedicta Ward, SLG, ed., *Daily Readings with the Desert Fathers* (Springfield, Ill.: Templegate Publishers, 1988), 43.

the desert. Instead, we're called to find ways to emit the same hospitable silence that the desert gave us, offering only the great quiet as the testimony of our transformation. We're called to allow the space of deep quiet to so penetrate our personal space that others who cross over into that space are held in the peace, until that same peace and deep quiet can permeate their own souls.

- To begin this prayer practice, find a place where you can spend thirty minutes or so in a place that's quiet and relatively free of distraction. You might choose your own desert place, or a place in nature, or a holy sanctuary.
- Spend a few minutes centering yourself in the space you've chosen, and let your breathing be the assurance of God's presence with you.
- As you settle yourself, try to recall the details of one of your own desert experiences or practices that you've tried. You might re-read your journal from that time as a way to give focus to the various movements within you as your spirit met God's Spirit in the profound stillness of the desert.
- Close your eyes and imagine that you stand in the center of a large circle. You can see your body standing there, your heart beating, your nostrils breathing, your mind moving with thought, your soul searching for holiness, your feelings filled with passion and, at times, pathos. You can see that you are a complex creature and that the cells, atoms, sinews, bones, organs, blood, thoughts, feelings, and spiritual longings are in constant motion within you. Notice the energy that seems to keep that complex creature in perpetual motion.
- Now begin to imagine that the energy is slowing and coming to a place of rest and tranquility. The blood still flows, but gently, the scattered thoughts are finding their way into union, the feelings are gathering together in a meld of peacefulness, and the breath is slow, steady, even.
- You notice that as you become quieter and more still, that stillness begins to seep out in ripples throughout the circle that surrounds you. As this happens you become more and more "one" with the

circle, until there is little left but a great space of divine quiet and peace.

- Now, think of a person in your life you'd like to share your desert experience with—perhaps someone that you know is going through some difficulty, stress, or struggle in his or her own physical or spiritual life. After you've identified someone, firmly place his or her image on your heart and soul.

- Imagine that your friend, hardly aware of your presence as a separate, physical human being, steps into the great circle with you. You can feel your friend's presence and complex energy disturbing the settledness inside the circle. You don't feel a need, however, to speak or act to calm the disturbance. It's enough for you simply to remain at peace, and allow your friend to find the way in the circle of silence.

- The longer your friend is in the circle, the less and less disturbance you feel, as if the complex energy moving around in your friend begins to slow and you notice that the stillness begins to seep out into the circle, just as it did with you.

- You become aware that both of you have become a part of the divine soundlessness and both of you have experienced the healing of God. You shared the sound of God through silence rather than through words, and your friend drank that silence and found it to be the nectar of heaven.

- Offer a prayer of thanksgiving to God for the power of silence, sound, and sharing.

CHAPTER 14

From Holy Company to Community

⟨leaf ornament⟩

Its common name is tumbleweed. When a desert wind picks up, and it rolls across the empty landscape, it more closely resembles its other name, "wind witch." Traveling tumbleweeds look like giant cat toys and you half expect to see even larger fearsome felines running behind them to catch them in their great paws. These skeletal balls of twigs—a bit of a nuisance at times—share a characteristic element of desert life. The dry and twisted, seemingly dead tumbleweeds begin life as grassy succulent shrubs that seem full of the promise of life. After the seedling has unfurled and reached for the sun, green flowers burst out on the bush with abandon. By autumn, however, the plant has reached full maturity, completed its flowering cycle, and begun to dry out from the heat of the searing summer sun. Special cells in the stem allow the plant to break away from its roots so that it can begin its random roam across the sand. Amazingly, as it scoots across the landscape, this apparently lifeless rolling ball spreads seeds with every rotation. Each tumbleweed has nearly 250,000 seeds that are released as it rambles along the dusty ground. What looks like a dead sphere of spiny branches is actually filled with potential life. The hard desert existence that denuded it of its lively and youthful appearance, leaving it an empty shell of stripped spines, actually gave it what it needed to go through the world as a harbinger of life.

When we find ourselves craving delicious, delectable, decadent solitude and we scurry off to the desert for a taste of what we crave, we're surprised that the solitude can feel difficult and unfriendly. If we resist fleeing the difficulty and unfriendliness, we gradually come to understand that we're not alone in the solitude—the company of the Holy One is as undeniably present as the warm breath that filters through the air passages of our nostrils. Awakened to that real but quiet presence, we relax and begin to feel that the solitude won't swallow us up. The immense solitude seems to shrink down to our size, and when its borders are within viewing distance, we're assured that we belong—somewhere, to Someone, for all time. Little do we know that we'll become like the "wind witch"—denuded of our hopeful juvenile possibility, scorched of our sassy and attractive soul clothes, left looking and feeling like a pile of fossilized bones.

As unlikely as it seems, it's not happiness and hopefulness that make it possible for us to share the wonder of life with others. It's having been through the crucible of desert heat and desert death. When we can enter that vast and empty terrain with nothing but the hand of God to lead and shape us, we're exposed to the pain without which no one can truly understand the gift of life. As deadened as we feel after our experience of solitude in the desert, like the "wind witch," we've been prepared to be a herald of life in the world through which we travel.

There was a time when God's people had gone through just such a desert experience and they felt life had been stripped from them. They had no moisture in their souls, no hope in their hearts, no connection with what mattered most. The prophet Ezekiel had a vision in which God put him into the midst of a plain that was filled with dry bones, as lifeless as God's people felt. God asked Ezekiel if he thought the bones could live. Ezekiel had the right answer: "Only you know, Lord!" God told Ezekiel to proclaim the words of God to the bones and when he did the bones came together, and flesh and muscle grew on them. Then God told

Ezekiel to prophesy to the wind, and the wind came from the four corners and breath came into the bones that had taken on flesh and muscle so that they lived. This was God's way of assuring those whose souls were arid and faint, whose hearts were frightened and forlorn, whose lives felt isolated from the breath of heaven that life would not only be given them again but that they'd share that life with others when they were brought back into their own land. But it was the arid heat of the desert that fired their flesh and left them aching for moisture and breath that would make it possible for them to return to their own land different than when they left.

There's a reality about the desert that can't be averted or even missed. That reality is so inhospitable that we'll do almost anything to avoid it. It's the simple truth that life is only fully known and fully shared when we've embraced the pain of desert solitude and been visited by the hard company of the Holy One. We don't need even to enter what felt like a geographical wasteland to claim this truth. What we need is to release ourselves into the hands of isolation, loss, and pain as they occur in our lives. We've all encountered such desert landscapes as these in our lives, and if we're honest, we know that we've become proficient at finding ways to cover-up, deny, and distract ourselves from their pain. Yet they hold for us the solitude that has no edges, the company of the Holy One that is both comforting and unrelenting, and the opportunity of embracing and sharing life in a way that is so authentic it's disarming. Deserts take away our life and give it back to us again.

I remember a time when my life had become crazy with all the demands and expectations of others. My life was so full that I had no time or energy left to listen to the silence of my soul. I had become little more than a well-oiled machine, a machine that would eventually quit working altogether if I didn't stop the frenetic pace. I knew I needed to step away from that craziness to enter desert solitude. I was unafraid of the edgeless nature of that solitude, and I even looked forward to the Holy company I knew would dry out my tender shoots and leave me feeling vulnerable and exposed. I reveled in the dawn that grew from night's shadows, the heat that left my tongue as parched as a stone, the dullness of the topography that forced me to slow my energy, the starlit sky that invited me to peer inquiringly into the heavens. At first it was the solitude alone that grasped my soul and seemed to feed it with the manna that is nutritious if not tasty. After some weeks, I began to feel the stroking of my soul that alerted me to the fact that I wasn't alone, and my focus shifted to the steady presence of the Holy One. Then I began to revel in the disturbing energy of God that left me quickly filled but hungering for more, the unnerving truth that my soul had gotten lost beneath a crusty layer of falseness, and the unwelcome reality that God wanted nothing less than my whole self. I was content to spend whatever time it took to fully immerse myself in these spiritual revelations and I had no sense that that time would be short. Yet, when I least expected it, I was called away from the desert to attend to the needs of a loved one. I struggled with the decision about whether to go to my loved one or stay in my desert of solitude, but my better nature won out. What I remember most from that time was that I couldn't take as much time as I thought I needed in order to experience desert calm, desert healing. I had insisted on a desert respite, but the demanding life I left was not going to go away, just because I had decided to take a desert sojourn. It wasn't long before the voices called me back. Leaving before I was ready—before either the desert or my own soul had released me—left me feeling horrible with bottomless grief. Surprisingly, it was one of the greatest losses I'd ever known. Often I'd left the desert for the activity of the world, but never before had I felt that I was being coerced back to activity in such a way that I felt I was losing the desert—losing God—losing any hope of life. I wept and wept when I left, and I felt that my sobs would cut me in half, so unready was I to leave. I wasn't through with the solitude and unprepared to be snatched away from the place upon which I relied, the place that was tending my overwrought and out-of-shape soul. My deep sorrow left me feeling that I was little more than a dry, dead bone. The pain seared but releasing myself into it made it clear that the breath of heaven hadn't left me. I was alive, and the solitude I'd endured, the holy company I'd encountered, would make it possible for me to roll across the days of life in the active world, spreading the seeds of life that had been given to me while I passively woke to the desert sun and slept under the desert moon.

It can be difficult to return to community after having undergone the fierce isolation of the desert. It can be a rude re-entry that leaves us feeling pummeled and raw. Even when we're ready to get back into the "thick of things," we can find that the bustle makes us edgy. When we expect that we'll enter the community and nourish those in it with our experience, we may be bitterly disappointed that no one is interested. When we feel so transformed by our desert experience that we can offer something valuable to the community, we may find no meaningful outlet for our experience. We know we've been changed, and we want to be a part of the change in others; indeed, we feel compelled to make a difference as a result of what we've learned about God and ourselves. Alas, we don't impact our community with our teaching, our words, or even our actions. What grabs their attention instead is our willingness to be blown about by the wind, randomly dispersing the seeds that have accumulated in the leafless twigs of our soul. The word *community* comes from the Latin word *communis*, for "common or general". Our intense desert experience hasn't made us unique or distinct but has prepared us to meld into the common, general framework of life. Another of the great gifts the desert gives is the lesson that when everything is stripped away we can begin to accept our true nature. We can begin to embrace our anonymity. We can taste the nectar of true humility. We can accept that we're novices in life with no claims to arrogance or pretension. We can just be a "wind witch"—a tumbleweed that empties its life on the sand with and for others.

A Prayer Practice for Moving from
Holy Company to Community

Nobody ever teaches us to be humble. We're taught to make our mark, to stand out from the others, to show our prowess, our strength, our uniqueness. We learn to strive for the highest position in the company, to acquire the trappings of success, to spend energy and money to look like movie stars and models. We can end up living an "all-about-me" life, convinced that we need to set ourselves apart from anything that's ordinary. We find ourselves alienated from the fabric of life that in its very commonality is a complex tapestry of loveliness. The solitude of the desert and the rough company of the Holy One can awaken us to that complex loveliness by showing us the part we have to play in the rhythm of life—uniquely ours and yet not distinctly different from anyone else's. We begin to find our peace not by making our mark but by making our place. We begin to find our meaning not by standing out, but by standing close. We begin to find our truth not by following other people's truth, but by knowing our own. As the wise thinker Ronald Houston once said, "No light is needed to see the truth because the truth is the light." Let this prayer practice help you to dwell in that truth that is the light.

Begin by setting aside an hour and choosing a place where you can be near the earth. You might go to a park, or sit on a sandy beach, or lie on the side of a slope. If you can't go to a specific place, use your desert place, and try to bring something from the earth into it—a rock or a branch, for example.

- As you settle yourself in, spend a few minutes becoming aware of your breath and God's presence in your breath. As you breathe in, imagine that the Creator is giving you the breath of life, and as you breathe out, imagine that your breath is joining with all other breath in creation. Breathe in the breath of life; breathe out into the breath of creation. Breathe in the breath. Breathe out into the breath. Breathe in. Breathe out. Breathe.

- Take several minutes noticing your environment, paying attention to the details. Pretend you've taken a photograph of it and are now looking at that photograph. Like the childhood game of taking a picture and trying to find the hidden clues in it, look for the hidden beauty in the space. What makes it a complete picture? What would it look like if certain elements were removed? How would it feel if only one or two things were dominant? Where is the light? Where are the shadows? Where is the darkness? How does the mixture of color and texture flow to create the feeling of the whole? How does the smallest element contribute to the cohesiveness of the space? Where is there distortion? Where is there fluidity and peace?

- Now, close your eyes and imagine that the space is no longer filled with the things of earth—grass, flowers, sand, water, twigs, trees, rocks and stones—but with people. Again take a few minutes to notice what the space feels like with the people in it, by considering the same questions as before.

- Record your reflections of both meditations in your journal.

- So far, you've been a keen observer of a space. Now, participate in the space. First, imagine yourself wandering into the photograph that comprises creation. What happens? Do you disturb the scene, or meld in with it? How does your presence affect the beauty of the whole? How unobtrusive are you? Do you find yourself feeling like a stranger? Do you want to walk quietly or somehow alert others to your presence? What do you add that was missing before? If someone else were taking a photograph right now, what impact would you have on the picture? If you were taken out of the photograph, how would the viewer of the photograph be affected?

- Now, imagine that you've become a participant in the space filled with people and reflect on the same questions as before.

- Record your reflections in your journal.

- One of the most profound ways of understanding and experiencing the beautiful in the common is to listen to the simple musical tones of monastic chant. One of the distinguishing aspects of monastic chant is that no one voice stands out. The monks are trained to modulate their voices to become one with all the other voices. The unity of the voices is what creates the tone that is so simple that it can soothe the most distressed or anxious soul. Life can be coming at us in waves of tumult, and monastic chant will bring a sense of utter peace and tranquility. Spend the final minutes of your desert time listening to a recording of monastic chant and find the ragged edges of your soul being soothed and smoothed. Offer a prayer to God for your part in creation, and ask for the grace to play only that part—simply, humbly, and beautifully.

CHAPTER 15

From Emptiness to Fullness

It's a familiar postcard image for the Southwest deserts. An old gold miner outfitted in ratty jeans, scratched and dirty boots, tattered shirt and ragged leather vest sporting a sweat-filled, dusty, stained, and misshapen hat walking alongside his burro through the sandy barren landscape. The burro, laden with every supply and mining implement possible, looks as if he's out on a Sunday stroll, while the old miner looks like a tired and worn-out bum, weary of the sun, yet unwilling to give up his insatiable penchant for gold.

As a young child, I was bedazzled with the seeming mystery behind finding gold in the desert. I lived near an old gold mine that had layers of legend surrounding it. Because the mine's location was a secret, it attracted tourists, ne'er-do-wells, and amateur gold diggers who would boldly, and sometimes foolishly, make the difficult trudge into the mountains with nothing but a greedy hope of finding the flashy mineral. Many of those adventurers perished under a cloud of mystery: lurking bandits, legend had it, guarded the mine and killed anyone who came too close. The reality was different and less mysterious: people with little knowledge of the desert, and even less knowledge of desert survival skills, probably just succumbed to the bitter and unforgiving desert environs. As a child, however, I loved hearing the stories, and each time a would-be gold miner was carried out of the mountains dead, I'd resolve to someday find that mine. While many urban amateurs found their end in the hot desert, countless other prospectors, looking just like their less fortunate brethren, had spent the whole of their lives in those treacherous desert mountains. They intrigued me and whenever they came into town for supplies, they fueled my youthful fantasies of finding glittering fortune in the mountain mine.

When we first go to the desert eager to empty ourselves of all that's left us feeling like a pot of soup about to boil over, we're immediately relieved that the flame underneath us has been turned down and we've settled to a slow simmer. As we accustom ourselves to the desert rhythms, even the simmer slows until we feel breathlessly still. Our frenetic life fades into the background and rests in our consciousness as hardly more than a distant memory. When we cross into this region of inner calm, we begin to find that our soul hungrily soaks up the healing and restoration it's been offered. The longer we remain in the still and expansive space, the more willing we are to experience true emptiness and to be filled with the light and love of the Holy One. The Holy One responds faithfully. Our souls are fed, tended, and readied for a return to daily life. When we know it's time to leave the desert and re-establish ourselves in our workaday lives, our souls are excited about the possibilities of our return. The desert has given us a renewed enthusiasm and energy for life, and we want to express that enthusiasm in fresh and profound ways that will make a difference in us and our world. Consider, however, what life is like when you've been sick and in bed with a fever and flu for several days. At first, your body releases all the toxins that have been building up in it. When your body is left wasted, empty, and weak and you've slept more than you ever thought you could, your fever breaks, your appetite begins to return, and you realize you're "on the mend." After the initial symptoms are gone, you may feel as if you've been born all over again. You're happy to greet the light of day and anxious to get out, breathe the air, exercise, get back to work, or even go to a party with friends. But if you try to return to your normal pattern too soon, you can very quickly find yourself right back in the bed. The body needs to pace itself as it returns to wholeness and strength. A desert experience is much the same.

The danger to our soul lies not in the place of emptying ourselves of the toxins built up in us, nor in claiming the reality of complete emptiness, but in how we live out "fullness" once we return to the rigors and demands of our regular lives. As energetic as we feel, we must ask ourselves, "What difference do we want to make? To whom will we make it? What will be the effect on us? How can we maintain our fullness if we give it away to others? How will we keep our sense of peace and wholeness in the midst of the complexity of life? If we don't give attention to these questions before our return, we'll find that our desert experience fades all too quickly, and we're simply reinfected with the toxins that drove us to the desert in the first place.

As intrigued as I was as a child with the crusty leather-skinned prospectors, the burros that accompanied them were equally fascinating. It seemed incomprehensible to me that a 350-pound lumbering mule could survive the harsh conditions and the relentless heat while carrying around a heavy load mile after mile. I suppose that's also why I've always loved the story of Balaam's mule saving his life. God was frustrated with Balaam's continual openness to the request made by King Balak to curse his enemies. As he went, the angel of the Lord stood in the road to stop him. But it was the mule, not Balaam, who saw the angel of God and actually prevented Balaam from following a path God had not laid out for him (Numbers 22:1–41). Over the years, I've found that the hardy and resilient burro can be a spiritual touchstone, particularly as we shift from desert isolation to the world of society. Wild burros were brought to the southwestern deserts by Spaniards in the 1500s because of their toughness and ability to withstand the arid conditions of the desert. Not only is the desert devoid of all but the slightest moisture and as hot as a sauna, the ground is usually rocky and uneven. Wild burros, though, are amazingly stable on their feet, even while carrying heavy burdens through hot, dry environments. While they need to be within ten miles of a water source, they can lose up to thirty percent of their body weight in water without any negative effects and, what's even more amazing, can replenish all they lose within about five minutes of drinking. On the other hand, human beings losing only ten percent of their body weight in water become so severely dehydrated that they need medical care, including several days of intravenous liquid replacement, for their bodies to be restored to balance. It's easy to see that a wild burro will withstand the desert aridity and barrenness long after an exhausted prospector has died of thirst.

The bumbling burro, such a common sight in the Southwest, can teach us at least three things about returning to our life in the world after a solo sojourn in the hot sand. First, we need to be within close proximity of a watering hole. In other words, we need to have spiritual oases nearby that will give us the moisture we need when our soul feels dry. We need to know where those watering holes are, and we need to be able to get to them quickly and regularly. If we wander too far away from them for too long, we do so at our spiritual peril.

Second, we need to know when we are in need of a drink. When the woman with a hemorrhage secretly touched the hem of Jesus' garment, he knew that power had gone out of him. Jesus kept an eye on his soul, taking its pulse and guarding its condition. He knew its movements—what nourished it, what depleted it. Too often, it isn't until we are at the brink of spiritual collapse that we realize we've given too much of our fullness away without seeking replenishment. Like Jesus, who was so keenly aware of his soul that he knew when power had gone from it, it might be wise for us to be attentive to the amount of our spiritual fullness we can afford to lose before we become so dry that our soul becomes weary.

Third, we need to be realistic about the difference we expect to make. Living in a culture that prizes a strong work ethic, we're often more concerned with quantity than quality. We can be so compulsive about making a difference in the world that we lose sight of the fact that we don't have to carry the load for every prospector in the desert. To be effective, or spiritual, or worthy, we don't need to carry everyone on our back through the dusty, hot trails of life. We're not responsible for everybody. Like a female mule who gives birth to only one burro a year, we might make a difference in only one person's life this year. But if we can do it with the fortitude, commitment, perseverance, and stability of a burro, that will be plenty.

The desert stands ready to allow us to empty ourselves in its immensity, to teach us what it means to be truly humble, to provide the space where our soul can be filled with the Living Water, and to energize us to return in that fullness to give a drink to other thirsty travelers. When the desert has given us these great gifts, she asks of us only this—to keep an eye on the condition of our soul, to guard God's most precious gift to us.

A Prayer Practice for Moving from Emptiness to Fullness

It's difficult to guard our soul when we're edging our way back into the pattern of life that waits for us when the dawn breaks through the pink sky, consumes our energy through our waking hours, and takes us to the point of welcoming the hours of darkness and sleep. When we are wiling our hours away in silence and anonymity in the desert, we are keenly aware that our soul is being given the nourishment that not only satisfies but keeps it constantly in the presence of God. The water of heaven drips freely and silently into us, but without careful attention, we're likely to stumble and find that what we've gained has been spilt all over the place. It can be an accidental stumble or a gradual slide that occurs because we haven't been watchful. When our body tells us we need moisture, we get the message. Our mouth feels like chalk, the image of liquid passes across our mind, and we can't think of anything but getting the water we know we need. We grab a cool glass of water and, if our thirst is severe, we gulp it down without a breath, as if we're filling an empty gas tank with gasoline. As the water is dispersed throughout the screaming nerves of our body, we perk up, ready for what comes next. We may not be as attuned, however, to the signs of thirst in our soul. In much the same way, this prayer practice can help us discern the movements of our soul and learn what to do to guard its preciousness.

Select a place of quiet where you can be alone for at least thirty minutes. The place is less important than the assurance of being relatively undisturbed. Before beginning the practice, find a beautiful jar or other receptacle that you can bring with you into the space. This will become a metaphor for your own soul, so look for one that you feel is particularly meaningful to you, or that has some unique characteristic. Take your journal and your jar to the desert place you've chosen, and after settling yourself and becoming aware of any tension or anxiety in your body, close your eyes and become aware of the space where your body is placed.

- Take a few moments to feel the quietness of the place, and the silence of God's presence around you. Become aware of how your breath moves into your lungs, filling them with life and emptying that life into the space around you. Notice the steady and equal filling and emptying that occurs without thought or manipulation. Offer a prayer to God in thanksgiving for the miraculous balance of your breathing.
- After you've centered yourself in the presence of the Holy One, hold your jar and become familiar with it. Feel its texture, notice its colors, its shape, its pattern, its simplicity, and its flaws. Make some notes in your journal about the jar. Why did you choose it for the prayer practice? What makes it special to you? What has been its history with you? Is it new or old? Did it belong to someone you loved before it came into your hands? How would you feel if it were broken or lost? What has it held inside its walls? Who has taken what out of it? How does it resemble your own soul?
- Now close your eyes and pretend that the jar is a visible and physical representation of your soul. Imagine placing the jar in the hot, sandy desert where it will be filled with the gifts that God is ready to give it. As the jar—your soul—sits under the warm, desert sun, notice how ready it is to be filled. It doesn't try to coerce or

choose or manipulate or control what God will give it. It simply waits, humbly and expectantly. And without the barriers of self-conscious manipulation, God is readily able to give it what it needs and to fill it to the brim, nearly to overflowing.

- Now imagine that you've gotten up, walked across the sand, picked up the jar, and placed it back in your lap. How does it feel now? How careful do you feel you need to be with it? How will you share its contents without spilling everything out at once? How will you know when the jar is being depleted? How empty will it need to be before you bring it back to the desert place?

- After recording your reflections in your journal, take a few minutes to be aware again of the steady balance of your breathing. Filling, emptying. Emptying, filling. Each filling is important. Each emptying is important. Each one occurs without any effort—only gift, pure gift. Thank God for the life-force of your breath and for the time you've spent together.

- End your practice by slowly reading the following lines from my poem "Monastery Grace":

. . . The wind sounds gather now.
I hear because I am silent.
I breathe the moistured gust,
Breathe out the blood-warmed breath.
In sacred stillness my soul
Is draped with the richest grace.[9]

---

9. Renee Miller, "Monastery Grace" (2004; unpublished poem).

CHAPTER 16

From Release to Sacrifice

The best things about going to the beach in the summertime are kicking off our shoes, feeling the cool wet sand between our toes, etching our foot's imprint into the damp grains and watching the surf erase it a few seconds later. But best of all is searching for seashell treasures the tide leaves behind. We can find them in tourist shops, but we're always looking for our own special shell to carry away with us to remind us of our journey to the sea. Secretly, we may even be searching for a shell with a gorgeous cream-colored pearl inside of it.

Going to the desert provides a similar pastime, but rather than kicking off our shoes, we don a pair of boots and begin to tramp through the hot dry sand, searching not for shells, but for rocks. Local trading posts, of course, have every possible mineral available for purchase—from the inimitable "fool's gold," to shiny cold-black hematite, misty rose-colored quartz, or flaky mica the color of gold. The minerals and gems come rough-hewn, as if they were scooped out of the sand just minutes before, or tumbled and polished, show-ing off their finer and subtler shades of color. We can buy the tumbled ones by the handful to drop into a leather pouch, or we can just choose one, with a special word engraved into it. As attractive as the smooth and shiny stones are, they can't compare to the geodes that usually stand apart in the display case. On the outside, geodes look like unattractive miniaturized pockmarked planets. But a stunning and mysterious treasure lies within them—the most beautiful, even breathtaking, delicately colored crystals that dance in myriad patterns in the light. After looking at the price of the larger geodes, most desert travelers, like beach bums, take to the sand to find their own rough-hewn rocks, hoping they'll find their own geode with an exquisite inner treasure.

It takes thousands of years for the crystals in geodes to develop, and those semi-transparent sparkling crystals would remain forever hidden in their unappealing shell if they weren't cracked and broken open. A rough rock half-buried in desert sand will never display its unique inner secret as long as it just remains half-buried in desert sand. Life has a way of leaving us feeling, at times, like we need to be half-buried in a protective embrace—the embrace of God. We flee to the desert because it's always so ready to take us in and hold us in that embrace. We feel safe in those desert arms and slowly, almost imperceptibly, our soul begins to grow more beautiful inside us. We know intuitively that it's impossible to be in the Divine Presence and escape our soul's alteration. Through the twin movements of the heat of divine love and the cooling answer of human response, our soul, over time, is shaped and formed with the same magnificence as crystals in a geode. As we submit to the action of God within us, we come to depend on the security of the divine embrace and prepare to be released from that embrace into in our native environment. Like the geode, however, the mysterious loveliness of our soul can remain forever hidden unless—and until—we're cracked and broken open.

The very word *sacrifice* has an acrid taste about it. It can bring a choking feeling as prickly as a parched throat scratched by desert grit. We avoid sacrifice whenever we can, because we associate it with pain, loss, and discomfort, or with surrender of personal power and control. For centuries the sacrifice of Christ has been one of the predominant defining themes of the Christian faith. Yet skeptics, seekers, and serious believers alike are now questioning why such a sacrifice was needed. If God is a loving God, why was it necessary for Jesus to be falsely accused, betrayed, beaten, denied, and crucified? Any God who would demand such a sacrifice is at best, capricious, at worst sadistic. Any such God is unworthy of worship, obedience, or love.

Perhaps our understanding of sacrifice is too narrowly defined. The word *sacrifice* is rooted in the two Latin words, *sacer* meaning "sacred," and *facere* meaning "to make." In some fashion, sacrifice makes an act sacred, rendering it special, holy, unique, and setting it apart for a greater purpose. Like the crystals that transform the geode from a useless, slightly ugly rock, Christ, cracked and broken open, made both life and death sacred. He showed in the core of his being the undeniable truth that the soul belongs both to heaven and to earth, revealing that behind the exterior of betrayal, pain, even death, a holy reality transcends the ugly, despicable, and evil. Through his sacred-making act, every human being was given the opportunity to know that there need be no separation between heaven and human, between our souls and the heart of God.

When we enter the desert's embrace and God prepares us for release, there's always a purpose. We're not merely passive riders on a carousel of pleasantly painted horses going round and round through the days of life until the ride shuts down. The desert teaches us that we were created to show forth the wonder of our soul and to make things sacred. But it's difficult to embrace sacrifice. We are so accustomed to thinking that sacrifice will always involve the pain and suffering characteristic of Jesus' sacrifice that we can't imagine how to make anything sacred through our sacrifices. We don't even want to try to grasp the notion that only when we're cracked and broken open can our soul sparkle so gracefully in the sun that it changes those who see its beauty. When we detach ourselves from the ingrained notion that sacrifice always involves great suffering and despair, we can think creatively about cracking open the outer shell of our lives to reveal the splendor of our souls. We can begin to consider what it might mean to be sacred-makers in our everyday lives.

As the day of my ordination approached, I wondered how prepared I really was. I'd been longing to do what I felt called to do, but I knew that first I needed to get away from the sound of human life and go into the dusty, hot terrain that was my touchstone with the Holy One. I took my trusty blanket, drove to the edge of civilization, and walked with eager steps into the desert wilderness. When I was sure I was far from human habitation, I opened my blanket and plopped myself down on my knees under the hot June sun. I heard the sonorous desert sounds, felt the charged stillness, drank in the dry, bitter air. I prayed. I waited. It came to me quietly and slowly. As excited as I was for the ceremony of ordination, I realized that I'd never really wanted my life to go in that direction. Even though I'd made the commitment as a child to serve God for the rest of my life, I suddenly understood that the call of God had been, for me, always a sacrifice. The road to the priesthood was littered with red tape. Seminary had been a sacrifice. Now, ordination would be a sacrifice—tinged all around with beauty, glory, and light, but a sacrifice nonetheless. It wouldn't be a sacrifice of pain, a physical death as Jesus had experienced, but it would be a sacrifice of helping to make sacred the life and call I'd been given, whatever that might mean for me. In that desert space, God released me to make my unique life sacred in a new way. This was my chance to say to God once again, "Yes. Yes. I am willing to be cracked and broken open so that my soul may be on display for others, and so that I can be a part of sacred-making in a fresh way. Yes. Yes. I am willing. Yes. Yes. I accept the sacrifice." When my heart had ended its prayer of acceptance, I folded up my blanket and made the trek back to the car, to the world, to my ordination.

We go to the desert to be embraced and quickly find that the itchy aridity of the desert can leave us feeling as if we've been depleted of the very life we came to find. But, in that tender and demanding embrace, we're given the grace to relax—to be released from the embrace to do what our soul has silently known all along it's meant to do. As we prepare to leave the desert, we drop our defenses, no longer afraid to be a sacred-maker. And, oh how astonished we are when we're cracked open and our soul, turned crystal, blushes like the first ray of sun on a desert morn.

Prayer Practice for Moving from Release to Sacrifice

In the midst of the open space of the desert, under the sky that is so large that our meager eyes can barely take it in, the colors are shaded with faintness and sharpness at the same time. Stillness thunders throughout the cells of our body, the sand and rocks scintillate our soul, and we realize that we ourselves are encompassed in a cocoon of crystal holiness. As we settle down into the topography as seriously as a mourning dove flattening herself in the heat of the day, the revelation unfolds before us. The desert itself has made a sacrifice. Through the tumult of the ages, the flow of lava, the cracking of ground, she has made sacred a place that could easily be ignored by all but the most discerning. When we put up barriers in our lives that keep us from experiencing sacrifice, we deny ourselves not only the pathos that wrenches and rends us into wholeness, but also the possibility of becoming ourselves a sacred place where others are nourished and healed. So much in our world urges us to claim a happy equilibrium even when it shuts us off from the passion that helps us make our lives sacred. Books, prescription drugs, television, food, drink, shopping—all serve as distractions to keep us from staring sacrifice in the face. But imagine how our lives would be inspired, awakened, and made palpably real by bowing to the reality of sacrifice, and entering into it with every fiber of our being. This prayer practice provides a way to look into the window of sacrifice and find there not an onerous and fearful part of life to avoid, but a meaningful path for living an authentic life.

Set aside at least an hour, take your journal, and go to a silent place that is bare and lacks stimulation. It would be best to choose an old church sanctuary, a meditation room, or the desert place you've created for yourself in your home. As you sit in the space, notice its bareness and look for the subtle beauty a stark place offers.

Bring your awareness to the presence of God in the space and observe how much easier it is to focus on that presence when you're not preoccupied with the clutter of familiar distractions. Offer to God a prayer of intention that in the stillness of this profound presence you'll have the heart to discern what is beyond physical sight.

Close your eyes and imagine that there are two windows in the room. Each window is framed with filmy curtains begging to be parted to allow the air to flow freely and to display the picture beyond the glass. In your mind, pull your chair up to the first window. Stand and gently pull back the curtains. As you look out the window you notice that you're watching yourself during a time of painful sacrifice in your life. Watch yourself for a few moments, giving attention to as many details as you can about that time in your life—how you felt, how your body looked, what your responses were. Come away from the window, and sitting back down in your chair by the window, take at least fifteen minutes to reflect on the following questions, allowing yourself to release any emotions that rise in you.

- What was the sacrifice you remember from that time?
- How alive did you feel as you suffered pain or despair?
- What emotions charged through your soul during your time of trial?
- What did you do to calm the piercing pain?
- In the isolation of your despair how close were you to the Holy One?
- What were the threads of sacredness sewn together from the sacrifice?
- How were your compassion, your forgiveness, your clarity about the true essentials of life deepened?

Sit in stillness for a few minutes to allow your emotions to calm, and thank God for whatever grace you found from that time.

Now in your mind, go to the other window in the room and as

you pull the curtains apart and look through the pane of glass, you see yourself again. The scene that plays before you is a time in your life when you said "yes" to doing something that felt like a sacrifice to you, but didn't involve any physical pain, suffering, or despair. As at the first window, watch yourself for a few moments, giving attention to as many details as you can about that time in your life, how you felt, how your body looked, what your responses were. Come away from the window, and sitting back down in your chair by the window, take at least fifteen minutes to reflect on the following questions, allowing yourself to release any emotions that rise in you.

- What motivated you to freely make the sacrifice?
- Were your emotions both fearful and expectant?
- How did your soul grasp the truth that your choice would require more than you felt able to give?
- In your acceptance, and in your weakness, was the Holy One putting protective arms around you?
- How were you able to become a place of sacred territory that attracted others?
- How were you given the wisdom you needed to navigate your way through unknown terrain until holiness showed her sublime face?

Sit in stillness for a few minutes to allow your emotions to calm, and thank God for whatever grace you found from that time.

Spend the last minutes of the hour recording your reflections in your journal. End the time with a prayer of "yes" to the Holy One to be a willing sacred-maker in the life you have been given.

CHAPTER 17

From Belonging to Inclusion

The sun was only just wiping the sleep from her eyes to prepare for another day of light-shedding. Even though her warming face was not yet fully visible, the heat that hadn't dissipated in the darkness, still held in the desert breeze, brushed against the land and against my face. I raised my eyes to the mountain so stolid in the not too distant horizon and watched as the first rays of the lit orb made their entrance across the stage of the vast sky. As beautiful a panoply as those first rays are that stretch in geometric forms across the blue firmament, I was transfixed not by them, but by the mountain. Silent. Still. Wise beyond language and image. Appearing passion-less, but poised between heaven and earth, bridging both, connecting both, including both.

From a distance a desert mountain looks like a solid mass of rock and sand, displaying shadows only when clouds and sun meet in opaque formations. There's no indication that caves, crevices, caverns, and cliffs are hidden within the ancient rock and slippery sand. There's no witness to report that what's concealed from a distant onlooker is a secret of untold worth. That secret, so silent and hidden in the diverse texture of the mountain, is that there's no separation between earth and heaven—no lines of demarcation, no edges that split and divide, no harsh distinctions that keep heaven disconnected from the world of rock and sand, the landscape of body and soul. The desert is always fierce in this proclamation.

The mountain that seems to grow out of the earth has its apex in the atmosphere just beyond our reach. As our eyes ascend to that apex, our sight goes naturally higher and we wonder if the mountain that lacks speech is somehow alerting us to the fact that the separateness that pushes like an unwelcome intruder through the door of our psyche is just that—an unwelcome intruder. We're used to thinking that we're enclosed in a world of staccato, unconnected beats where the hope of union with heaven is something to look forward to at some future time, but impossible to experience now. As we robotically—even wearily—tread the dust of earth and encounter the daily limitations of our humanity, we know for sure that we're separated not only from one another but also from the One that breathed us into being.

Scripture is replete with images of mountains—many of them in desert landscapes. When Moses ascended the desert mountain surrounded with the cloud of God's presence, God and Moses conversed. In that textured place heaven and earth met and lines of separation were discarded. The mountain was the link between the two worlds; it became the place of union. The sight was fearsome to those who stood in the distance with upraised eyes, because it seemed incoherent to them that the lines, the edges, the distinctions, that made their life sensible, might not be as real as they'd thought them to be. It's one thing to wish for a direct line of communication with the Divine, and quite another to actually find that it exists.

It was in the midst of the texture of a desert mountain, in the still whisper of silence, that Elijah heard the heart of heaven and was given the strength to return to what felt like a wasteland, to take up the duties of daily life once again. The return to the call and mission of his life was possible precisely because the experience in the mountain had shown him that separation between earth and heaven was merely a necessary human construct adopted because of the difficulty for the human mind to grasp the edgeless-ness of eternity. We tend to define our identity by focusing on what makes us unique from others and then we try to fit our uniqueness into the uniqueness of everyone else. With this approach, however, we miss the eternal truth that our own unique identity and belonging are really a part of the entire "whole" that has no contrived boundaries.

It was on a desert mountain that Jesus was transfigured. The light of heaven, so bright it confused and blinded the disciples who looked on, was the ultimate signal that all is included—enclosed— in the infinite and boundless heart of heaven. The disciples, unable to comprehend the breadth of such inclusion, wanted to build booths. They wanted to make compartments. They wanted to draw lines and borders to make sense of the experience. Whenever truth is larger than our imagination, we want to systematically group and pigeonhole things to avoid the terrifying feeling that we're just a grain of desert sand lost in the midst of the enormity of a reality that threatens to swallow us whole. The desert mountain is there to remind us that it is just such a truth as this—the truth of inclusive union with the all-ness of eternity—that can actually make us whole.

In one of my most recent desert sojourns, the real estate agent who sold me my condominium took great pride in saying that it had both a lake and mountain view. Of course, any view at all tends to help sell a property. Views of water are particularly attractive, but what sold me on this small dwelling wasn't the blue lake in the midst of the desert landscape, but the mountains that are ever-changing and ever the same. I was at a period in my life when I'd come away from work that had sizzled my soul as surely as the desert sun sizzles an egg on the sidewalk in summer. I *desired* to be isolated from other human beings. I *felt* isolated from the God I loved. I *was* isolated from my own true self. I wanted to draw boundaries around my life so that I could not only retain my isolation, but also insure that I could also retain my own personal drama. I distanced myself for some time from everyone and everything that was not absolutely essential. Like the disciples, I was safe in the "booth" I'd created for myself because I was so certain the lines and distinctions would stay in their proper place. I knew I needed to rediscover my identity, I knew I needed to reclaim my belonging. I had no idea, just then, that I simply needed to revise my perspective and trust in the truth of eternity. When the shades of darkness were parted to make room for the light, I would sit in silence on my balcony, staring at the mountain that felt so close I thought I could reach out and find its sharp rocks scraping my skin. I looked for signs, watched for shadows, envisioned the Divine One meeting me in that mountain. Later, when the brightness of day shifted and the intense light was brought down a notch, with the dusky vapors of orange and nearly orange slicing across the desert sky, I'd again sit silently on the balcony staring at the mountain. Even though I avoid exercise at all costs, the time eventually came when I knew that the mountains were luring me closer. So, I left my balcony for the open desert and headed in its direction. Many days I would sit at the base of the mountain and let my spirit be carried into its crevices and caverns. It was the deafening silence and sheer size of its solid enormity that held me and transformed me. After several months sitting with my desert mountain companion, my sizzled soul began to cool, and I began to glimpse a sliver of the grand surprise that the only real answer for my disordered uneasiness was recognizing the fact that isolation is, at times, a part of life, but need not define life. As long as I could feel the earth below my toes and stretch my eyes toward the mountain that called me even higher, I'd be included—enclosed—in the open space of eternity.

When life has hardened our hearts with a crust that isolates us, the desert day dawns yet again, and the light blithely pirouettes over the far-off mountain, and the silent mountain calls to the soul, "Come," as it once called the young disciple who had just traded in the city for a desert cell:

Alone and implacable, almost from before time, the mountain stood. The tiny crevices and gaping canyons told silent stories of life in the shadows of solitude.

The young disciple stood at a distance fearful, yet lured by the mystery of that silent mountain. How she loomed—so stately, so strong, so much larger than he. Yet, she beckoned the disciple with her mystical beauty. Such solitude and beauty, if succumbed to, could overpower him. Deep within he knew this. But his eyes could not look away—his heart could not break free from the embrace.

In just the moment that he began moving closer to that which called him, he heard the voice of the voiceless. The mountain, so far from having the ability to sing, provided a home for that which could perform a nature aria. He closed his eyes for just a brief second and heard music that quickened his heart and made it dance. He opened his eyes and looking upward caught sight of the music-bearers—small bright-winged creatures who sang the song of God.

"Ah," he said to himself, "solitude is not always silence."

Unafraid he advanced toward the mountain.[10]

A Prayer Practice for Moving from Belonging to Inclusion

Desert mountains are holy places where we can acknowledge the infinite truth that all of creation is forever connected with God. Nothing stands outside. Nothing is lost. Nothing is isolated from eternity. Of course, communication with the Holy One occurs in all kinds of ways, in all kinds of places, but the mystery of mountains seems to create a gateway for human and divine encounters that can be so tangible they become etched in the context of our life, and even leave their trace on the hard rock of the mountain face itself. We are accustomed to hiking up and down mountains, using them as playgrounds in winter's snow, or being awed by their majesty amid an otherwise unremarkable terrain. We have less experience with approaching them ready and willing to meet and speak with God. We do not expect to enter into the imposing silence of a mysterious mountain and suddenly be aware that the presence of God is palpably near. We are content to focus on the entertainment

---

10. Renee Miller (2000; unpublished).

value of mountains and, in so doing, miss seeing them as meeting places of heaven and earth.

Begin this prayer practice by setting aside at least one hour. Going to a mountain would be ideal, but if you can't, choose a spacious, quiet place, or go to the desert place you've created for yourself. If you can't physically go to a mountain, bring a mountain to you by finding a picture of a mountain that appeals to you. Look in books, magazines, or on the Internet for a mountain large enough to capture your imagination and mysterious enough to entice your soul. Make a copy of the picture to take with you to your place of prayer. You'll also need your Bible and journal.

- As you enter your place of practice, take some moments to center yourself in that space. Notice the sounds, the scents, the feelings within your own body. Pay attention to the pattern of your breath. Is it labored and quick or steady and even? Acknowledge to yourself that, for the next hour that you will be in this space, your breath is free to slow and move as gently as air flowing through a desert mountain canyon.

- Become aware that this time and place are filled with the divine sparks of the love of God. Offer a prayer to God of your intention to be fully open to the encounter that will occur and of your desire to break free of all boundaries that keep you separated from God, yourself, and creation.

- Spend a few minutes doing a pairing exercise. Write the following twelve pairs of words in your journal, leaving space between each pair for writing.

Light	Dark
Female	Male
Love	Hate
Sky	Sea
Desert	Forest
Animal	Air
Black	Snow

Leaf	Angel
Rock	Blood
Eternity	Presence
Death	Food
Cloud	Fire

- Consider the aspects of each pair of words by reflecting on the following questions:

What separates them?
What are their edges and boundaries?
What are their similarities?
What would happen if their edges were less defined?
What would happen if they merged?
How will they look in eternity?

The first few pairs will be familiar and provide easier reflection, while the later ones will require more thought and imagination.

- Now, let your heart and eyes be drawn to the physical mountain before you, or to the mountain picture you've brought with you into the prayer space. Familiarize yourself with the mountain. Look for its shadows, its crevices and cliffs, its tiny caves that provide shelter. Notice how the mountain appears to rise out of and be completely formed of earth, and yet seems to reach to the unseen heavens. Observe how large and enigmatic the mountain seems, in comparison with your small frame. Notice how the light plays off the jagged rocks and the smooth walls. Become as familiar with the physical aspects of the mountain as possible.

- Open your Bible and slowly read through the mountain encounter between Moses and God as recorded in Exodus 19:16–20. Close your eyes and, putting yourself in the place of Moses, try to reimagine the scene that you have just read, letting the mountain before you, or the mountain in your picture, become the mountain described in Exodus. What does it feel like to climb the mountain in the midst of the thick cloud, the smoke of fire, the trembling rocks and sand? What words do you want to speak to God? What does God say to you in response? How do you know when God has alighted on the top of the mountain? What excitement and/or terror do you experience when God tells you to come to the top of the mountain for a meeting? What are your thoughts as you make the treacherous climb? What do you feel when you are perched between heaven and earth, in the presence of the God of heaven and earth? As you record your thoughts in your journal, ask God what you should know or understand from this reimagining of the scene.

• Bring your practice to a close by standing and raising your arms up as high as you can. Feel the "grounded-ness" of your body on the earth, and your longing for inclusion in what is just out of your visible sight. Thank God for the connection between the dusty sand of earth and the clear air of heaven's breath and ask for the grace to dwell fully and inclusively in both.

CHAPTER 18

From Light to Life

In the midst of the desert landscape that looks so drear, drab, and dead, we find the pulse of life. What we call "life" is often merely a substitute—an inadequate, unreal, lackluster substitute—more dreary, drab, and death-like than the dull monotony of the dry, desert land. What we call "life" is often no more than a mask that covers the true life that is wild and passionate, sometimes uncontrollable and chaotic, as blood-red hot as the sand that litters the landscape in the scalding heat of desert sun. We want to tame that life force because it's unpredictable and we're afraid of its power. A regular, routine, controlled, unsurprising existence may be boring, but it is safe. The desert will never provide this safety. The desert will never create an environment that allows us to settle for what is not life. The desert will never protect us from the pathos of real life so that we can continue breathing but not truly live. One of our first impressions of the desert is that it eminently dull—as unexciting and lifeless as our daily existence sometimes seems. As filled as our lives are with activity, friendships, goals, problems, vacations, errands, children, family, hopes, and dreams, we still might feel that our lives are unexciting and lifeless. It seems the desert is playing a joke on us when it insists that we wake up to the color and texture of our own life, while it displays its beauty precisely in its boring, monochromatic bareness. In reality, it is not a joke at all. Rather, the desert is so richly raw with life that anything that is less than real life is immediately shown to be an impostor. Going to the desert, then, is a risky business—not only because of its climate, but because it will expose our flat lives for what they are and insist that we claim life in its fullest, most real expression. We'll never be able to deeply encounter the desert without having to examine the details of our ho-hum lives. We'll find that life plays out before us as it was created to be—demanding our entire engagement, energy, and enthusiasm.

Other topographies nourish and replenish the life we've become accustomed to. The ocean, for example, can help restore our balance in life. A forest can help cool the heat in our life. The mountains can help restore our hope in life. A field of flowers can help restore our sense of playfulness in life. An open plain can help restore our sense of the possibilities in life. The desert, however, scratches at our life, skewers and rotates us over and over, as if we were a desert boar being turned on a spit, until all the debris has been singed away by the fire, leaving us with a relentless thirst and a glimpse of death. Then, in the silence of our pain, the night stars gather. They hang like rare gems in the sky, and we are held securely in the darkness until the dawn peeks up over the horizon, and we know that we want life—real life—not a facsimile of it. We know, however, that the choice for such a life is a dangerous choice. It is unknown territory and we are unsure that we have the proper skills or methods for coping with such a feral existence day in and day out.

Though it's rarely been my experience, there was a point in my life when I wanted to be taken out of the desert. I wanted to escape from it because I felt broken by its random wildness that throttled me with truth and reality until I felt I could no longer stand. I craved an even existence—a life that resembled a smooth tan-colored trench coat, than a nubby-weaved coat of many colors. Why did the desert have to be so uncompromising and unremitting in its burning away of the dross that had collected around my life? Couldn't she just offer a kindly invitation to look at the more ragged edges of life and try to include them as well into my reliably patterned and structured life? Why the demand to "forsake all" and claim, instead, a life that rattled the emotions and stirred the soul without restraint? Couldn't there be a little mercy, a little understanding, a little acceptance of my boring need for stability? But as much as I desired to flee, I couldn't leave the desert at the time. Her arms of embrace hadn't released me. The darkness had descended, the light hadn't emerged, and unbeknownst to me, life was actually being happily reconfigured. With my escape routes blocked, the only possibility for me was to learn to adapt to the desert in order to survive long enough to reach the point of being able to claim that newly reconfigured life. I had to take my lessons from the birds and mammals of the desert that, because of the extreme temperatures and paucity of moisture, have had to find ways to accommodate themselves to the environment in order stay alive and even flourish.

One of the first lessons I began to learn was to befriend the darkness. Many reptiles, rodents, and four-legged creatures indigenous to the desert have adapted to the environs by becoming nocturnal. Darkness is their friend. By resting in the day and foraging through the darkness, desert creatures protect themselves from the severe heat and retain the moisture critical to their sustenance. We're so used to sleeping when it's dark that we miss the treasures that the darkness offers. As much as I wanted to break away from the gloom of night that threatened to snuff out every last remnant of joy, I came to see that the darkness of the desert was my ally and would, in the end, be the means whereby I retrieved my verve for life.

I also learned that I needed to go deeper down—deeper in. When the heat of the blistering sun crackles even hard stones, the desert animals burrow into deep holes where the ground is cooler and not so exposed to the scorching sphere. When the very underpinnings that have kept us completely unaware of "real life" are being systematically eroded, the last thing we want to do is enter more deeply into the depth of our human pain. We want to stay near the surface watching for the next possible exit. Near the surface, however, we risk being fried. I came to understand that the deeper I was willing to go into the pain the desert had given me, the more able I'd be to drive the fear away.

I learned, also, to seek shade. Even in the empty desert, with its sparse vegetation, there's always some sliver of shade. When the desert reveals to us our life, or lack of it, we feel like the heat of that revelation will sear us until we are no longer recognizable. As much as we want to avoid an unsightly encounter with our possible misshapen self we can develop a familiarity with pain that makes us unwilling to move forward. We want to weep until there are no tears left, so that the truth of what we've suffered will not be lost from our memory. The desert mammals have understood that such prolonged presence in the intense heat will ultimately destroy. Shade must sometimes be sought. When I felt that my life was being played out before me in a way that I could not begin to comprehend, I wanted to be soaked in the searing ache until there was nothing but my soul left shivering in the sun, but I had to learn that dwelling too much on the drama of the heat of sadness would ultimately destroy any chance I had at real life. I needed to search for shade from time to time, to catch my breath, to cool my skin, to ready my soul for the gifts of the desert day.

But, the most critical lesson I learned from the desert creatures was to soar on higher air. It is, of course, the ground that receives the ferocious desert heat. The rays of the sun bear down on the sandy earth, drying it of even the smallest amounts of moisture. The ground radiates the heat the sun left behind and releases it into the air. Desert birds have adapted to the heat of the earth and the heat of the air by soaring on higher air. They fly higher where the air is cooler to retain the moisture their bodies need. When the desert seems to have warmed our lives to a boiling point, we can feel trapped, not only with no way of escape, but without the proper tools for lessening the heat sapping every ounce of strength from us. This particular stay in the desert, for me, was like that. I was being held, almost against my will, and I had no known way of reducing the flame that made me burn. Then I remembered the desert birds.

The air is cooler up above. It was as if the heat that seemed to be so haphazardly assaulting my life, was telling me to look upward—to soar on higher air. I was reminded of the lovely passage from Isaiah 40:31: "but those who wait for the Lord shall renew their strength, they shall mount up with wings like eagles, they shall run and not be weary, they shall walk and not faint." When I lifted my soul to heaven's gate, I found that even the most severe pain has fringes of hope.

When we are willing to relinquish what is less than a vibrant life, we come to find a life we didn't even imagine existed. When the desert's seeming calmness erupts into a clamor, we want to switch our moccasins for sneakers and sprint from the desert's heat and beat. As perilous as the desert seems then, we are in more peril by sprinting away. The desert darkness *will* lead to light and the light *will* lead to life, but if we run too quickly, the passion that makes life real will elude us. Imagine, instead, letting the desert rip and rend, reveal and release, renew and restore. Imagine being a desert creature who learns how to adapt to the rugged desert clime and in the ruggedness finds a life that is as beautiful as the soft shade of amber spreading across the empty sky as the heated desert returns to nightly slumber.

A Prayer Practice for Moving from Light to Life

Sometimes we don't notice the monotony in our lives. It becomes crystal-clear, however, when an unexpected crisis occurs, or when our energy is depleted, or when we can't imagine doing anything any different, when the smallest changes in our environment seem to disturb us. The physical desert pounds the blandness from us in strong and dynamic ways; somehow the thorny cacti, the rough lava rock, and the endless beige sand bring us to an awareness that passion has gone out of our lives. And, while part of us will always avoid the unpleasant and the unanticipated, these very "deserts" offer us the canvas upon which to rediscover the fervor of pulsing life. For the first part of this prayer practice, set aside thirty minutes and go to a coffee bar or restaurant, where you'll be in the midst of conversations and activity. Take your Bible and journal along with you.

- Center yourself in the presence of God by becoming aware of the holy energy that throbs in the sounds and beating hearts that share the room with you. As you hear the talking and laughter, see the shapes of the people and the textures of their clothing, try to sense the power of breathing in the place. Each person breathing in, breathing out. Your own breath moving rhythmically in and out. Notice how the breath is the Divine sign of life. Thank the Holy One for the breath of heaven that infuses each person animating them into living beings.
- Read John 15:1–11 slowly and attentively. Linger over the words and phrases that seem to cause your soul to tingle, and after reading, record those words and phrases in your journal with a short description of how they moved you.
- Turn to a fresh page in your journal and say a silent prayer over the page asking God to move your spirit and your hand as you do a drawing exercise. Try to suspend your natural inhibitions toward drawing. This exercise isn't intended to produce a work of fine art, or even haphazard art. It's meant to help you enter your life in a more visceral way to reflect on the "realness" of the life you're living.
- Draw a wild tree—the wilder the better. As you draw be aware of the feelings swirling through you. Notice the randomness that sometimes comes from your writing implement, as well as the predictable and careful pattern you try, at times, to sketch. Think of each branch that you draw on the tree as an aspect of your life, and reflect on the following questions:

How connected is the branch with the other branches, trunk, and root system?

How do you feel when you draw a crooked or otherwise misshapen branch? Do you try to straighten it out, or do you let it be what it is?

How much do you want to domesticate the arbitrariness of the branches and leaves?

Where do you feel chaos in the tree, and in your own life, and how does that chaos stir up passion within you?

How deeply do you draw below ground, how high to the sky?

- After you've completed your tree, imagine what it would look like if it were planted next to a tame and well-manicured tree. If you could choose which tree would represent your life, which one would you choose and why?
- Re-read the passage from John 15:1–11, looking frequently at the tree you've drawn. Close your eyes and ask God if there are any insights or ideas you've missed. Be still for several minutes and record any reflections in your journal.
- End the practice by becoming aware again of the energy around you, the holy breath that fills your lungs and flows unimpeded all through the room, and the wild cacophony of life that is embodied in each human being. Offer a prayer of gratitude for the gift of life and ask God for the grace to live the life you have been given with attention and intention.

Epilogue

The desert lake rises to the edge of a charcoal gray butte, and if I were to climb to the top of the butte, it feels like my next steps would be to heaven itself. The mountains behind the butte seem only half-there, and I fear that were I to step off the butte, I would be entering another dimension, another existence. As the sun slowly rises, the butte turns nearly black and the sun's rays shine only beyond the furthest misty mountain. Above, the clouds begin to disperse as they try to clear the way for blue sky and yellow sun. My soul is drawn to the distant mountains; I stretch toward them, lurch toward their mystery. There, I know the cloud of God will encompass me. There, I know I'll be welcomed and embraced, leaving behind all the tawdry, pressing, urgent concerns of this world without the slightest whisper of regret. In the absolute peace of that heavenly world, my soul will rest and be completely still.

When first we go to the desert, we bring with us all our hopes for fixing the imbalances in our lives and bringing sense out of the chaos that continually seems to scuff our soul. We prepare as best we can to encounter the wonder and beauty of a land that can seem hard-hearted and harsh. We look forward to the isolation and the time that will be completely ours. Whatever hopes and desires we bring to the desert, however, will pale when we're actually there.

We'll be suddenly aware that we've stepped off the butte of our busy lives into a world so unfamiliar, so unlike anything we know, that it seems as if we've entered another dimension of existence. Once our initial feelings of excitement and exploration have faded, and the implacable land continues to stretch empty before us, we'll begin to smell danger. We will begin to feel as if we're falling from a precipice without a net to catch us. In the instant that we become aware of the possibility of the menacing threat of annihilation, we'll find ourselves behaving like a roadrunner—"taking to the road running" as fast as we can, away from what we sense will consume us.

Roadrunners are a kind of cuckoo bird popularized in cartoons. The rather large body of the roadrunner prevents it from staying in the air for long, so it flies only when danger is breathlessly imminent. Mostly roadrunners scoot through the desert by walking and running—up to nearly twenty miles an hour! Its quickness on the ground makes it a formidable hunter and a difficult foe to attack. Adopting the tactics of the roadrunner might, in fact, remove us from the encroaching fear, but what we came to the desert to find can only be given when we refuse to use our legs to get us out of the environment that seems so alien. Instead of "taking to the road running," we are asked to "take to the sand sitting." We are asked to remain resolute in silence and submission to wait for the desert to dispense her lessons in her own time and in her own way. We're asked to wait until the heart of heaven opens to us through the heat of earth. Inevitably what the desert gives us is not at all what we thought we came to find. We're taken to a reality beyond the scope of our everyday lives. The desert invites us into what looks like a barren place and in the barrenness we find a fullness we could only have guessed at. That fullness doesn't come easily. It doesn't come on our timetable. It doesn't come in predictable patterns. It's revealed, instead, as quietly as the emerging dawn, as slowly as the going down of the hungry sun, as dramatically as the shadowy mist on the morning mountain, as simply as a shaft of light on a shard of clay. If we are patient enough to "take to the sand sitting," we will be emptied of everything that is unnecessary, and filled with the manna that only heaven can provide. Whatever is unattractive or unappealing about the desert experience at first glance is later discerned to be so rich, so deep, so full, so needful that we are amazed that we ever even considered "taking to the road running."

As unfamiliar as most of us are with desert landscapes, we do know the desert terrains of life that have been seemingly thrust upon us, against our will, when we felt least ready for them. These inner deserts, even more than the physical desert environment, require us to "take to the sand sitting." In the sometimes harrowing experiences of such deserts in life, we are given sips of cooling water from the hand of heaven, and the thirst we didn't even know we had begins to be quenched with heaven's nectar. If we cannot go to the physical desert, we need never despair, for the desert will always come to us, and whenever we are held in its rough embrace, we will be both broken and healed. Rather than praying to be spared the desert sojourn, we might pray, "O God, call me to be still before the void and open every layer, every fiber of my being in readiness for You—not how I imagine you, but You Alone."

Whatever else can be said, let me end with this. Every time we glance over the mysterious butte of the desert horizon, we can drop confidently into its depths and "take to the sand sitting." Always—always—always we will be surprised that in the whirl of terror and grace our trembling fingers have reached upward and have grasped the silken thread of heaven's dress.